I0560184

More than a Gathering

More than a Gathering

Reflections from the
Poets @ Artfest 2023
poetry festival

an anthology

Editor: Bruce Kauffman

First Edition

Wet Ink Books
www.WetInkBooks.com
WetInkBooks@gmail.com

Copyright © 2024 Wet Ink Books
Copyright © 2024 Authors

All rights revert to the author. All rights for book, layout and design remain with Wet Ink Books. No part of this book may be reproduced except by a reviewer who may quote brief passages in a review. The use of any part of this publication reproduced, transmitted in any form or by any means, electronic, mechanical, photocopied, recorded or otherwise stored in a retrieval system without prior permission in writing from the publisher or a licence from The Canadian Copyright Licensing Agency (Access Copyright) is prohibited. For an Access Copyright licence, visit: www.accesscopyright.ca or call toll free: 1.800-893-5777.

Title – More than a Gathering

Editor – Bruce Kauffman
Cover Design – Richard M. Grove
Layout and Design – Richard M. Grove

Typeset in Book Antiqua
Printed and bound in Canada
Distributed in USA by Ingram,
 – to set up an account – 1-800-937-0152

Library and Archives Canada Cataloguing in Publication

Title: More than a gathering : reflections from the poets @ Artfest 2023 poetry festival : an anthology / editor, Bruce Kauffman.
Names: Kauffman, Bruce, 1950- editor.
Description: First edition.
Identifiers: Canadiana 20240381580 |
ISBN 9781998324095 (softcover)
Subjects: CSH: Canadian poetry (English)—Ontario—Kingston. |
CSH: Canadian poetry (English)—21st century. |
LCSH: Canadian poetry—Ontario—Kingston. |
LCSH: Canadian poetry—21st century. |
LCGFT: Poetry.
Classification: LCC PS8295.7 .K56 2024 |
DDC C811/.6080971372—dc23

I'd like to dedicate this anthology to all of those who took part in the 2023 poetry festival, both onstage and off. To Artfest Kingston for their ever-welcome of it into their own each year. To my publisher, Richard M. Grove (Tai) for his excitement to see a collection come out of that event, and then for his equal care in design allowing this manuscript to become a book.

Contents

Introduction

The Power of Words to Take Your Breath Away
We're full of words. K. V. Skene
The fire that gives us the words. Linda Rogers

Dear Readers:

Aware that spirituality nurtures the body and saves the world and the future, and grateful that, no matter the season, art festivals and lit gatherings always bloom all over the world, we are now entering the pages of an impressive anthology, *More than a Gathering: Reflections from the Poets @ Artfest 2023 poetry festival,* that confirms a higher rule: the soul offers reason and beauty and it also *needs* reason and beauty.

Well-known artist, photographer, poet, writer and publisher Richard Tai Grove, and great poet and editor Bruce Kauffman, a Kingston literary mover and groover with his own poetry CanLit radio programme, have come together to muster a significant group of fine poets, who contributed their works for *Poets @ ArtFest ix*, a 2023 magnificent event. The extent and quality of their submissions made Kauffman and Grove, two tireless literary promoters, think beyond the ArtFest. That is how this remarkable anthology began to take shape.

Canada and Canadian authors are second to none in preserving art, literature — *culture.* The Canadian lit fountain is inexhaustible. A full list of Canadian poets would be difficult to compile, as much as it would be challenging to declare, direct a failsafe count of lakes in Canada's imposing geography: imposing is too the long tradition of poets who have been blessed with insightfulness and sensitivity to pour out their feelings as they see, hear, explore, discover, touch and depict Canada's immeasurable life force, and their inner forces, from their own perspectives and styles.

In my introductory words to my second review book, *A Shower of Warm Light* (QuodSermo Publishing, 2021), I commented about my second "journey": " ... *and visit once more in edifying alliance the enthralling, colossal landscapes of Canadian poetry.*" Thanks to Kauffman and Grove — and all the poets who honoured the book with their over 130 vetted poems — we have a new first-class ticket, illuminating and exciting, to the quintessence of a glorious nation that has deeply influenced the numberless themes poets have written about enriching the superb Canadian "PoetDom" [Poets' Kingdom] mosaic.

Humankind rose to prevail and language was paramount in our development and moulding of our universe. The title of my Introduction and the quotes I open it with (from two Canadian poets), tell us that words play a vital role in our lives. Skene emphasises that words are there for us, within and without, surrounding us, filling us; and Rogers makes it evident that there is this inside passion providing inspiration, complementing the compelling external motivations streaming into the poets' perceptive minds. With my title, I say that words, when sincerely and creatively penned, have enough potential to reach a peak where they spark the best of people's intellect and sentience, and give them pleasure.

But there is much more. Speaking of words, we are touched by Carolynn Kingyens's "The Weight of Words," a powerful, all-meaningful, very eloquent poem where a few lines superbly condense a million thoughts and messages. The way she begins generates enough anticipation:

"Some words bear enough
weight..."

Definitely, the poets in the book take the power of words up to another level. Sainte-Marie claimed that *"The job of a poet is to get information across in a way that's effective in making change."* (Taken from *Tamaracks: Canadian Poetry for the 21st Century.* Lummox Press, 2018. Page 38. Print copy. Introduction by the Editor, James Deahl. He refers the reader to Reader's Digest, Volume 191, Number 1,144. November 2017). While voicing their innermost urges, our poets pass on facts in poetic form aimed at producing change. This change will positively affect the readers'/listeners' thoughts, emotions, attitudes and worldviews.

Thus, evocative words are what editor, publisher and poets have, to take your breath away. But, not just *any* words; they are words that, in the poets' hands, acquire a communicative status where appealing beauty, cognition of the world, criticism, reflection, joy and sadness in their many-sided hues of meaning, and astute acumen, harmonize and substantially stir our humanity. Take, for example, Anne Archer's "Riversedge":

"... the space between
comfort and delight

like the right word
in the right place —

the world beyond
the rapids thick with crows."

Is it not what I am trying to explain here? Comfort and delight in writing, in feeling, in *sharing with others* what we write; the poets' apt words in the most fitting places, those places where they will cover broad audiences (a Poets' Fest!) — let's not forget the impact of the spoken word, which is accompanied by gestures, eye contact, interaction and the face-to-face unique experience.

Read now Alanna Veitch's "I See Miracles":

> *"Give me – the stories you dream*
> *while you wake in a world that exists, but*
> *not as I've ever known it*
> *Tell me – the tales of the day when*
> *you will wake here and relish the living*
> *we've had"*

We soon realize what the miracles are: it is the orality of the act of poetry reading; it is the storytelling, the urge for dialoguing and, again, the act of *sharing*. These poems were read — told — to audiences who listened in and absorbed the transcending significance of words soaring in the air, reaching their ears, alerting their minds, soothing their hearts.

Let's read from Carma Niceforo's "I don't Want to talk about the Weather":

> *"Are you sure you want to know me?*
> *I don't waltz gently into a person's life*
> *I slam into it like a truth telling tsunami*
> *Unintentionally destructive*
> *As I stalk down lies like I'm starving for stories*
>
> *And I'm not always right…*
>
> *… I can understand if you need to talk about the weather*
>
> *But I can't. Not anymore*
>
> *So if you want to know me.*
> *Then show me your scars."*

Wow! What a confession! What a way to speak out straightforwardly, sugar-freely! Wonderful poem. I can visualise the public's involvement, their synergic reaction and relatedness…

Underneath words there is enthusiasm and commitment; from these lines surface statements, "decrees," descriptions and confessions splendidly supported by imagery engraved by intense, devoted human beings. You will find exceptionally penned, passionate pieces.

Ponder Sue Bracken's

"This Love Poem Is for You":
"For you who held me through loss,
lifted me through joy, anchored my way,
surprised me with the small things —
a favourite drink, a favourite book,
a late-night cheese-and-onion sandwich.

For you whose touch is heat and keeps me young."

All these words honour Canada, Canadian poetry, and by extension each and every poet whose lines are a part of this Wet Ink Books anthology I am privileged to introduce. Let's toast to our poets, our anthology and our Canadian boon of vastness in geography and spirituality.

Relish, dear readers, a priceless *More Than a Gathering...* Under Kauffman's magical editing knack and Grove's perfectionistic fine-tuning, you and poets will unite in the truths rightly expressed, in delightful sharing, hope, confidence and enlightening growth. We need all of those, and Wendy Jean MacLean's "Becoming Hollow" reveals such need optimistically and elegantly, especially its last two lines:

"Fear, loss, love, joy worry me hollow,
but trees give me words for the loss
of my need to be full, and freedom
to trust the wind will write poems in my soul
even when I fall."

Associate Professor **Miguel Ángel Olivé Iglesias**. *BEd, MSc*
Professor of English as a Foreign Language,
Literature and Stylistics
Cuban President of the Canada Cuba Literary Alliance
Author, Poet, Writer, Editor, Lit Reviewer, Translator

Editor's Note

It happened the July 1st weekend, 2023.

The ninth in as many years and the seventh in person. It, in any of those years, was the much anticipated, from the start really, Poets @ Artfest outdoor, summer poetry festival held as part of the annual Artfest Kingston art festival there in City Park.

In 2020 and 2021, of course, we managed even to meet in the distance, say over the phone, or one-on-one recording sessions where we were socially-distanced in a convenient park. The work then shared within the virtual festival pages via radio and blogspace. But from 2015 through 2019, and then again in 2022 and 2023, we met LIVE in the park inside (and when the crowds grew so big, outside) our large tent there.

Many of the poets who attended every year were local, but roughly 1 in 3 each year were from places other than Kingston – always Toronto, Ottawa, Montreal, and then often so many other places between and beyond. And I have to say that each and every one of those poets in any of those years were wonderful. And each event dear to my heart.

My heartfelt thanks to all who have ever taken part in this event over those years. Not only those who were scheduled to read, but also those who attended the workshops, the open mics, the book launches that have been part of it, and came to listen, absorb, to feel the 45-50 poets each year who'd come to read. I do treasure each, and every one of you.

There was, though, something as if almost magical at the festival in 2023.

You could sense it, feel it. There was a special energy. And, of course there was that any year. And again much so in 2022, the first year we were back live – but even as amazing as that was, it was nothing like 2023. That event was mystical.

When I sensed it immediately there in the early morning that first day, I thought to myself, *Oh, it's just the incredible 'thing' it always is with this festival*. But then it seemed to amazingly grow, and when more and more and then more people throughout the three-day festival were telling me they'd felt the same thing, I knew it was more than my imagination. And occasionally we'd talk about how special it all was. And try to figure out all the whys of it.

Word of this reached a publisher I've often worked with in the past, Richard (Tai) Grove, Wet Ink Books. He contacted me and said, "Put together an anthology, and I'll publish it."

So, what you have here in your hands is the work of forty-seven poets, forty-three of the forty-five featured poets, and four poets who either read at the open mic session or attended the intuitive writing workshop.

And just yesterday, the 6th of April, 2024, as I was going through a final edit of this manuscript before passing it on to Tai to take it then down the publishing path, I think I finally figured out why things felt as they did last summer. As I write this, I remember two days ago, I came across a very poetic quote by T.S. Eliot. It read, "The purpose of literature is to turn blood into ink."

And I believe now, that over that three-day weekend there last year, as the poets read their own words of poetry off their pages, their words flowed through the open veins in the air, turning their ink back to blood.

Bruce Kauffman,
Editor.

Abbie Miolée

border

there is so much   to be grateful for
and still my heart is frozen in the negative –
still mourning   its severed attachments –
still searching   for home –
still warning   my scattered mind
not to ignore these signs
        and waves of awareness –
not to forget that I'm   an emotional being –
                not a machine –
my function   cannot be manipulated
        by any algorithm   amalgamated
            to control me
                because I am free...
except that   it is
        and I live in the fallout
            of a sacred awakening –
so unsure of myself   on the border
        of trust   and fear...
but even on the wavering edge   I can see
        so many blessings in front of me
and feel love   despite the boundary
    of distance –   feel secure
        even with severed   attachments...
somehow   I know   my heart
    will not always feel this hollow
        and I will heal
            by letting these feelings

                guide me.

rebirth

where trees die
mushrooms will grow –
all energy lives on
but we just may not know
that becoming closer to death
does not mean   the end is near
because love lies at the core
beneath layers of grief and fear
and only the open hearts
will fully hear
the symphony of life
so maybe   there is purpose
even in the war and strife
to empower   our compassion

all our bodies will decompose
into the same Earth
so to honour another
is to know one's own worth
because all lives   are intertwined
by an infinite common thread
and love   is the bridge
between the breathing   and the dead

just as mushrooms will grow
once spores are carried by the wind
after the ending
a new life will begin…

spinning

I wish I could understand myself
then maybe   I'd feel more sane
and find the axes
        that divide the cosmic planes –
                and if the lines that bisect
                        are also what connect
all the uncommon factors
                then maybe   the figures
                            are all significant
                        and too infinite
        to be considered
                                    a limitation...

I wish I could converse
with my future self –
                                    would she
                be wiser?
        calmer?
would she have learned   by then
                            how to let go?
and how would I know
        the joys of life
                without the promise of pain?

I wish I could decode   my intuition –
                            she only speaks
in the medium   of memetics –
the whispers   of rustling leaves –
the silence   within   music –
        and gusts of wind
                so strong   some days
                            I am reminded
of my inferiority   to this noisy world
        and the mathematics of Mother Nature...
                so still   some days
                            I forget
                                the Earth is spinning.

I will rise

somewhere
    beneath the imprints
        of my environment
I will find myself   and I will rise.
I will not second guess myself –
my intuition knows best –
            my wealth
is way more precious
    than paper   or plastic money –
it is the currency of love
        that flows through me
            like milk   and honey.
        this wealth is made
by balance –   not business –
    it will afford me   an escape
from this place   that suffocates me
        beneath the layers
            of false identity
I will find myself   and I will rise.

Alanna Veitch

I See Miracles

Give me – the stories you dream
while you wake in a world that exists, but
                    not as I've ever known it
Tell me – the tales of the day when
you will wake here and relish the living
we've had

I see miracles growing and thriving and dying
as the moon wipes the earth with her pale blue face,
and her eyes cast a lonely but lovely loon light
before morning awakens our earthly bodies

Lend me – the thoughts in your beautiful mind
that wrestle with me and my
womanly being

Share you – but most of all see
that I do just as the others
                    do

I see miracles growing and thriving and dying
as the moon wipes the earth with her pale blue face,
and her eyes cast a lonely but lovely loon light
before morning awakens our earthly bodies

Un/Interrupted

What is it to be un-interrupted?
not awakened from a transient state,
but rather resting here in silence

I sit – eyes closed – striving towards stillness;
escaping the sounds that crash against me
evoking images that touch and leave me
            different and the same

Interruptions that become, to me, a
private motion picture
parting, returning, and wanting to interrupt
indeed, *needing* to exist

To exist – what is it but
a series of interruptions?
Of forces that push and pull for attention,
            and oftentimes, more than one can give

But I do give
into the chatter that colours my vision;
into the scent of sweaty bodies and
sweet summer grass

And still – fighting towards stillness;
resisting the things that
make my heart beat, I
                        sense it all:

the rhythm of the credit machines
and gravel crunching beneath feet;
the birds chirping in canon; the bee
buzzing around my ear;
the children announcing their excitement to
their guardians nearby;
the smell of coffee and bubble gum vapes and
homemade cherry jam

The commotion invites me in – all
essential for me to be here
still   and   un/interrupted

June 12th, 2023

It was a rainy summer evening while wildfires
        raged in distant places
In distant places, but not so far for winds to carry
awareness of the devastation

Frightened, I stuff rags into the crevices
        of the window and door —
both connecting and separating me from
the world that lay outside

And, motionless, I feel emotional as the clouds
        that sit above me.
The clouds that weep with wariness,
travelling billows of angered concern

The mood was apocalyptic, and the air brown with dust
settling on door handles and windowsills —
dust I still have not washed off

Masked again, I think I must remember to wear a mask,
thinking of the places and people evacuating,
but unable to escape the debris

"What a sight!" I cry, stunned having noticed the sun — red
covered by soot, ash, and smog,
emoting a vision of suffocation

I was preoccupied by the minor troubles that befall me,
paralyzed by the tragedies
and my inability to aide

The night carried on, and the rain continued to fall
and, with it, I hoped that it would travel elsewhere,
where the summer heat smoldered,
        and nature called for some reprieve

Allan Briesmaster

Toward Finding

Somewhere subsists
the hidden plot
of bloom which lasts
a lifetime sought

whose gate (before
too late) one day
struck by a ray
will swing apart

as if that key
much as I'd stray
held straight in me
from the deep start

See Notes: 1

Windfor

Give me wind for my eyes.
They are so scaled –
not like fish but pipes perhaps,
or else too often calibrating,
hung unaligned, with weight of one
pan dipping down,
bent away from the other.

A constellation
of two is salvation
along the slide of the temporary.
Another like, also unlike, myself
to round my orbit and fill these eyes
with clear concern overturning
the screen of disinterest from
common reaches across common ground.

Let me open the lonely windows.
Let air, backed by the sun of your look,
circle in.
        Give us wind for our eyes.

See Notes: 2

Quantum Bio

"little, nameless unremembered acts" – *Wordsworth*

This life of contradictions wants no story
imposed on it, nor map to plot the days.
No catchall theory hatched, creating worry
over missed linkups. No spotlighted praise,
even well-earned, that sparks a trivial blaze
adrift through vast oblivious tracts of nights.

Offline from networking remote delights,
it opts for a more singular satisfaction:
upon fulfillment of one modest goal
after another unrelated action.

All leap or fall randomly to a dark whole
where constellated points and planes must melt,
becoming supra-spatially sensed. Thought, felt.
~ Waves carried beyond measure, pole to pole.

See Notes: 3

Amy Cadman

Resolution

The notion of three
A puzzle for me? Peut-être.
The answer is tree.

Bright

Breathe in. Digest
a smile. Breathe out. Share
with the world.

This Place

I write to find out
 what I didn't know I knew (Robert Frost)
I wrote my perfect day
 then I found it here with you
I feel you in the rain shine
 and I see you in the trees
Your heart flows through my spirit
 as you whisper in the breeze
I'm running to a birthday
 it's Canada's today
But first, do you remember?
 that branch is where we'd play
Your spirit's here; still present
 when your self is far away
We'll laugh in trees we climb again,
 Don't worry love
On blessed trips pray.

Anne Archer

earth   quake

Families harrow debris for signs
of life, air thick with names
of the lost, vowels tasting
of dust and blood and something
sweet, syllables, beloved
remains of prayer and hope.

Down the road, any road
another mother claws
her way out of the rubble
of home. Obsessive, compulsive,
manic words rain down on the space
between then and then and then.

Quake — what the shepherds did before
the star, the virgin, the baby, at
the sight, flayed by what they saw,
they journeyed home with a tale
on their lips, within the space
of another calamity, forgotten.

Riversedge

You're thinking of strawberries
or the wittering of hummingbirds,

the perfect stone, its edges
saucer-smooth so that it skims

plock, plock, plock
three times lucky and fills

the space between
comfort and delight

like the right word
in the right place—

the world beyond
the rapids thick with crows.

After life

On feast days, holy days, when
the stars are aligned, when over
the meadow just as light fades,
day shifts into night, and Jupiter,
Venus, and Mercury are in syzygy,
we set extra places at our table
for our dead, like our friend Stan,
who said the last time we were together
that a poem is a hand clasp
across a mutual loneliness.

So many join us now at these dinners—
my mother-in-law, for example, who
always pronounced 'squirrels' as 'skwarrels,'
she who would concatenate her rrrs
until they trilled. Until Alzheimer's
turned her into a hollow shell and
she had visions, Jesus adrift on
clouds of glory, though when
we would quiz her they were
more likely phosphenes.   Even

at ninety she claimed a brisk walk
twice a day was the cure for life's ills,
no time for gadding about, she had
her children, the grands and the greats.
Such a believer, she knew she would
be raised up, would join her husband
and the saints and martyrs in a heaven
above, forever and. Praise God from whom.
For all I know, the after life is a place dark,
cold, abyssalpelagic. Enough for me
that my dead warm the occasional poem.

Anne Graham

A Choir of Daffodils

I'm watching a choir
a choir of daffodils.
Their heads are turned skyward.
Does this stance enable their voices?
Because God is not up there
but sitting
here with me
on a chair
by the window
watching
a choir of daffodils.

Expectations

We are full of future expectations.
They are created by our own beliefs,
Which are both negative and positive,
Spawned by engrams of past experience.

This soup of presumptions, teachings, beliefs
is the birthplace of our dire predictions,
hopeful conjecture and darkest nightmares.
This witches' brew should be carefully strained.

Taste the soup of future expectations.
You may be surprised at the ingredients.
Savored they may form a new solution,
always add a heaping spoonful of hope.

What Love Means to Me

The question posed "off the cuff"
a subject, ignored or unspoken.
My heart can't stand it, and beats faster
as if to race time and prevent disaster.
Brain continues to puzzle the why's,
wherefores', the popular position.

Emotion is first out of the gate.
Cries like a baby, abandoned, lost,
seeking, sorting through the lies.
Brain argues "I love my children,
my world, the earth and skies.
My soul gently agrees.
Yet still the baby cries.

Armand Garnet Ruffo

Greasy Spoon

This is where we meet. Where
the cook behind the counter wears
a dirty white apron stretched
over a beer belly. The formica tables
and red vinyl chairs throwbacks
from another time. The room is small,
and I am glad because his voice is low
as if hidden behind heavy clouds.
A phrase of Ojibwe here and there,
I do my best to understand even though
he insists the language is in our blood.

He says we met a long time ago,
and I nod and pretend I remember.
He mentions names. Elders from
long gone. And my mind wanders
to Joy Harjo's poem about Saint Coincidence.
So many saints. So many coincidences.
When I ask him where he's from,
he drifts away as if he were the only one
in the room. His answer gets lost
in the steam rising from his cup.

He will later tell me about his life
on the street, drinking hard, jail.
He will go on about getting scooped
and put into a foster home. Just as
he will go on about a wife and children,
adopted parents, sacred teachings, and
learning to paint Woodland style from
Norval Morrisseau himself. It will
eventually be reported that much of it
he fabricated, stitched together
like the moccasins he wears.

Lunch Stop

over turkey and rice soup,
a smoked meat sandwich plain as day
I turned my head and there before me
was a forest of crimson hills
lunging over the Mattawa River.
the echo of timber
the thunder of men
moving massive log booms
beyond my sight
floating shanties
lumbering towards the Ottawa.

when I turned again
a young woman, maybe twenty-five,
was standing in front of me,
and I realized I had been travelling
and I told her.
she smiled politely and
poured me more coffee
and for the briefest second
autumn coloured her hair.
I said, ah ha! and she looked down
hard at me in my chair.

I was about to ask her
if she had grown up in the area
but she hurried away,
and I turned back to the window.
that's when I got to thinking
about the kind of strength it takes
for a young man to sweep
a young woman off her feet.
Or better yet the kind of strength
it takes – if that's what it is?
to cut and bind a forest
and send it down a river
without thinking twice.

Bethmarie Michalska

Stable Love
for Allison Macleod & Ian Thomson

The sheep dance, while birds flutter & tweet;
as we gather in Ashton Lane.

Undertaker's creaky stables morphed
to a drinking place for humans

"Take your libations up the rickety stairs –
Set *'it all'* aside"
to celebrate
a feast for upcoming   nuptials.

The cattle graze in fields,   farther out from Glasgow
Lowing at a distance
Noticing people's propensities
for cement.   metal   petrol   *noise*

Bovine huge, brown eyes blink in wonder
at city barns,
now wrapped in twinkle lights.
No hay
Yet continuing as places for food & drinks.

The mares   with foals still suckling,
appreciate   wild human passion
Get the reining in, that marriage brings-
Yet only after a fair time of prancing,
Galloping, & cantering on.

The couple's vows – solemnity & joy -
kilt & lace,   *roses showering* greenery.
Community hands holding – *heard promises*– high,
As the spouse's grin
forward embrace,
to start a ceilidh.

Sparse Paean*

"Hallelujah," as we come
from our homes or living rough.
Human hearts now gather round
Sharing joy and failings found.
Times of grief meet times of joy,
Clear, confused, our feelings soar,
far above our different grounds
making music's common sounds.

Through my voice I play with grace,
Find my calling here at last
Words and flesh rejoicing fly –
Feet on rock and heart in sky.
You have given me sweet gifts
Presence felt, my spirit lifts
Glorifying meeting You ,
Singing praise for others too.

We are one among the beasts
celebrating death's decay
Jackal, griffin taste with cheer,
Lions feast upon the deer.
Carnal knowledge feeds our fall
To compassion – with its toll
Still creation's bell rings clear:
"Death. Birth. Life. Ecstatic sphere."

Wakening worlds within without
Fugues abound o'er several paths –
Sweet alyssum's anthem sent,
Birch's ballad, oaks lament
Mountain's symphony resounds
Soul's own silence. Without bounds
Babbling brooks psalm sea's release,
Winds weep star ward sighing, "Peace."

*See Notes: 4

Pandemic Forest Bathing

Broken evergreen branches   dot
long limbs
climbing high,
trunks revolve with wind,
          at bases still.

Our feet tread   unsure
on sienna needles
covering hard ice.

We stroll where trees surround us,
Safe from urban landscapes,
Where coronaviruses spread.

Talk of vaccine's hope,
Trudge against mortality –
march breathing harder.

Speak of those we know who are sick–
Globally more than 115 million now–
in isolation –
of others who have died –
more than two & a half million worldwide.

Sigh of lost social pleasures –
Exhale such pettiness against immeasurable tragedy.

The pines look dead
upwards of twice our height.
Yet we take notice –
even much higher,
through scores of vertical scapes,
they live

beloved of the sky,
they'll rise to any pitch
to green.

Billie Kearns

Habit(at)

I come from Yellowknife and the Subarctic, the
Athabasca, my Mother. We know the smell of forest
fires in July, the flickering of the lights every time the
power goes out. We come from the moss, the
willows, the garter snakes, the fireweed, and foxtail

I tell home
        please don't forget me
        I'll do my best not to
        let myself forget you

I know where I come from
I can feel home growing
out of myself in every
hair through
scalp and skin
I pull it out
        recursively become
        home when I suck
        on the roots
        reteach myself
        how to speak
        to the land.

See Notes: 5

Auntie Energy

I brought Lana to Blue Rodeo last night.
I don't know that she liked them, but it seemed
like the thing to do. Whenever I'm going out
for a good time, I bring Lana with me
Blues Dancing, a party– bring that Auntie Energy
to keep me lively, to keep me Boss, to keep me laughing.

Lana was 6 ft tall or something. Big curly hair
and a wide smile that don't mess around.
I'm 5 ft 4 at best and always was a shy quiet girl.

My cousins picked out earrings for everyone
for Des, for Kookum, for Hopee, for Ash, for Beanie,
and Jamie, and we all bring Lana to her own funeral.
Pull up with her earrings, our braids, and Jamie is blasting
Boujee Natives in his pickup while we're all smudged
and crying in the two blocks we gotta drive to
Roaring Rapids Hall.

Uncle Johnny lights up the bingo board with her birthday.
Takes a pic. Tweets: *when your bingo caller dies*

I spend the morning listening to all the stories
about the Auntie I never really knew. Hearing stories
about the Auntie who I only realized still loved me
when we hugged one last time.

By the time 8PM rolls around they send the kids home.
Tell all the stories they shouldn't hear yet, play the slideshow
with all the party pictures. This may be the only funeral
I've been to with a dance party – a round dance to
Thunderstruck, Karaoke and Uncles tearing it up to
Johnny B. Goode. My cousin Cory teaches me to two-step
and the after party at Cathy's goes past 5AM.

So I know Aunties stay with us
after their hands have gone cold.
They still make sure the kids are
safe when they're spirits. The least
I can do is take Lana to this concert
to dance, and live it up a little.

Brent Raycroft

Sundowning

What did you teach me?
Don't say luck, say "If the devil doesn't
interrupt" or "Can't complain."
And if it's bad: "Just peachy."

Did he know
that to cross that bog from freedom into care
meant he'd lose his boots
and his words there?

Or that the TV'd play all day, on low.
Bland mnemonic of a time before he was alone.
No toast, no bread, no liquids.
Only gels and jello.

Did she know
when the heart attack hit broadside
she would get no further in the Binchy novel
bookmarked at her bedside?

Or that he'd live for ten years yet
and in the last forget he placed his fearful hand
on her cooling back, spine slack and
skin like wax.

May I outdo you, as you hoped.
Slink out of my room unseen and ramble
old but still noctambulant.
Tell the moon about you both.

Last Returns

for Tom Ivison

Movie posters had been papered over all the windows,
from within. I thought they were probably painting the trim.
When I pulled on the handle, though, the door was locked.
No chalk board on display. What time was it? What day?

Why choose to close so suddenly, no notice in advance?
In a later interview you'd say it would have meant so many
sad farewells with faithful customers. I'd be one of them.
Revenue might have surged, I guess, but to what end?

We might have gone out with a festival of modern European:
Bergman, Wertmüller, Varda, Wenders, Tarkovsky, von Trotta.
Or a batch of sentimental faves: *Persuasion, Magnolia, Babe.*
But the flicks I gripped in my hand were unspectacular that day.

The best was *Salting the Battlefield,* with the great Bill Nighy.
He plays a quirkily sexy civil servant and peace-loving spy.
Midnight Special starred Michael Shannon and Kirsten Dunst.
It doesn't make logical sense, but it's worth seeing once.

Last and least we sat through *Idiocracy,* a stupid movie
about a too-near future where everything is stupid
and where entertainment's been reduced to a bright,
chaotic stream of adverts for a sports drink with electrolytes.

Nothing to write home about — much less a poem — but in each,
I should point out, the criminals and specialists and idiots
who run the world had been defeated or at least embarrassed.
Movies do have happy endings more often than not.

One by one I pushed them through the old familiar slot
with the frowning face of Jimmy Cagney keeping watch.
I listened to the clatter as they landed, leaned in to read
the note you posted, and went home empty handed.

Bruce Kauffman

revisiting revisited

i sat in this café
22 years ago
many times
     doing this

     writing
       even then

this place called itself
something else
back then

people
time
days
years
decades
worlds
     all changed

but i sit here
still watching
ghosts   all
     the same

33 years on

at my journal

at a patio
        summertime

an evening

someone walking past
asked if i was drawing

i said   no, writing poetry

33 years ago and i
still remember this
        so lucidly

reminded here again
this morning
of that evening

and to this day still
am not sure
if they were
        interested
or
        disappointed
        as they walked away

a book

it will already
seem to be
opened for you
when you first
        see it

early on
you wouldn't have
even realized
        you were reading it

but you full well
have the book now
        and know it

you will fumble
across some of
        its pages

you will stumble
and even fall
        across others

but you will also
dance across
        many of them

you will be tempted
as you read
to open the book
        further

to that last chapter
        even that last page
and permit yourself there
to read a single word
        maybe even a line

but
you hold back

you understand it is
70 or 80 or even 90 or more
years long

it is your life

and each night
you close the book
        on the last page read
to be opened again
as you rise in the morning

it with all its wonder
and surprise
and not knowing
        within

Carma Niceforo

Snowdrifts

I used to find solace in snowdrifts
Tumbling backwards with arms outstretched
Into billowing clouds of crystals I'd sink
Spiraling into a drowsy descent
Until the world receded along with my ails
The stillness sprinkled with my quiet exhales
And gale winds whispering
Across the blanched fields

I discovered surrender in thunder
Freedom in lightening's uncontrived wanders
Frolicking to the vibrations of rage
I would dissolve myself in the rain
My skin inviting icy needles of pain
As the world grew lushly greener and vibrant
The echo of water drops
Transcended my silence

I found myself in the water
Challenged and chastised like her own daughter
I'd fight through the waves
The ice
And the stories
Through every season
At sunset
Through snowstorms
To cast off my failures and self limiting lies
My primordial self
Seen through my own feral eyes

Once I had accepted the stillness of grace
I would rise from the arms of Nature's embrace
Ready to meet the coming onslaught of malice
No longer in terror
Instead languid and liquid
Anchored by strikes in the ground and eternal renewal
I am empowered by forces
More potent than you

I don't Want to talk about the Weather

Are you sure you want to know me?
I don't waltz gently into a person's life
I slam into it like a truth telling tsunami
Unintentionally destructive
As I stalk down lies like I'm starving for stories

And I'm not always right

Inauthenticity makes me itchy
Since we're all running outta time
I won't talk about the weather
Just show me your scars
And I'll show you mine

Tell me
About the diamonds in your demons
And the beauty of your sins
That you still feel like you're 17
Even though you're exhausted

I want you to know that I see you
With my heart's sage gaze
Because your stories are the light
In the dark of my lost way

You see, I'm afraid I'm turning into a cynic
The sarcastic knowing in my vision
Is robbing my world of wonder
The Dis to Illusionment slicing
With a sharper blade than I thought it would

For me,
Illusions set ablaze have cast the darkest shadows
The way forward has required
A willingness to be scorched by the very light
You see by

I can understand if you need to talk about the weather

But I can't. Not anymore

So if you want to know me.
Then show me your scars.

Gaslight

They had me in this stuttered state
Of pattern interruptus
Like seasoned hypnotists,
I'd no chance to follow my thoughts
Explore my emotions or question the caught...

Voice within my throat

Unable to holler to dance or to scream
Because I was seen
I felt they were watching every little thing
My skin
crawling with resentment and agitated discontent
Even once beloved accents
Are now the vibrations that ignite my frustrations
Hollowed out by indifference and invalidation
With the steps of a sinner in supplication
My cadaverous spirit stalks affirmations....

Like they're lifelines

It's always opposite day, except it's opposite minute
No matter what I said I was always corrected
If I was allowed to speak at all
They taught me that
Down is up and up is down
That love is cruel and words are just sounds
They'd say
"Don't be so emotional, irrational, hysterical
It was meant to be satirical
Metaphorical, not literal!
The sky isn't blue, it's black as fuck
And you're not sad, you're just stuck
Let me tell you how to feel
And when you can react
I'll let you know what you can think
And how to act
And when to speak"

And then they'd watch me eat, watch me sleep
Watch me breathe, then watch me leave
Once a brief reprieve, they could not believe
That this time I left for good.

And although they bargained, raged and pleaded
Plotted, and manipulated
The pervasive truth invaded
My body into submission
Ripping the hinges off my prison
Sundering the friction, the facts from the fiction
Purging the violence from the silence
But
Like most wild things suddenly freed
I froze....

Overwhelmed by the horizon

Carolyn Smart

Revelation

When the surgeons cut him open
did they startle at his flaming heart?
They must have thought they'd found a saint
inside a velvet painting.
He would have laughed at that.

Yet his heart was so luminous
he once drove for two hours
to look for our boy who called,
crying and wandering the streets.
The boy didn't know exactly where he was
but said he was afraid and very tired,
his father was driving and driving
and suddenly saw him, it was two a.m.,
he was there, head down, walking.
His father pulled him to safety,
he cut through the night
and took him into his arms.

How did they find each other?
Drawn together in a miracle
through the Ottawa streets:
one ruined boy in a black hoodie,
one man driving a dark car,
heart ablaze.

See Note 6

For the two donkeys that live on Road 38

From the window of the car
we would see the donkeys
shining like chocolate
in the rich green of the fields.

They were standing close,
sometimes eating,
sometimes sniffing fragrant summer air.

They were doing their good work:
to guard the sheep.
How we loved to see them!

Their tails would flick,
their soft calm necks
stretch down into the meadow grass.

All that summer of your dying
they did not know the other work they did.

Needles

I learn Houdini's widow died
on a train from LA to New York.
Her body was removed at Needles.

When I think Needles
I remember a white cat in the desert sun,
112F as I stepped out from the car
and the air was a blanket,
thick, around seven-year-old me.
The cat did not move more than a flick
of its tail, its pink eyes fixed on the horizon.
We were driving across America
which they said was a bright, open land.

In memory also a boy with the last name Needles
who talked of stepping out onto the stage
with grownup men and women
and the bad things that happened out of sight.
I tried not to imagine, just flicked my gaze
across his eager face
so I could feel the heat of youth.

Lies, I often said to people in my life,
I am only telling lies. All writers lie.

Before he died, Houdini did not
tell the truth to his grieving wife:
he promised her the ultimate escape.
She was still waiting for his reappearance
as the train shuddered down through the hills
and a bright light came towards her in her dreams.

The Board of Directors
tours the Integrated Care Hub

We stood apart, a group in layered clothing,
our chins tucked down inside our scarves.
The winter came on fast this year,
reminding how the wind makes rivers on our cheeks.
Beside us was a group around a fire
drinking coffee, drying piles of clothing.
One eager woman held up her knit blanket:
the winter blew it back and forth like straw.
Then one young man stepped out the back door
and hurried past. I'd seen him in the sleeping pods
when I was trying not to pry. He looked so young
they'd need to ask his age to let him in.
I could not help but stare and caught his tired eyes,
his worn red face and hands. I hope he got some rest.
I watched him as he climbed inside his tent of plastic bags.
In the trees above, three crows were mobbing a fat hawk
and though they shouted in its face
it would not turn its sharp-eyed gaze away
from what it saw just waiting down below.

November 2022, Kingston Ontario

Carolynn Kingyens

The Weight of Words

Some words bear enough
weight to incite mass mobs
in closed spaces,
words like *FIRE!*
words like *He has a Gun!*
Imagine the people's panic:
their pushing and pulling
down, crawling
to the nearest exits for life.

Now imagine a naive girl
Who hasn't learned respect
for the weighty-word
never, who uses it
too loosely when speaking
like *I'll never do that*
to only do precisely *that*
And more.

After making anniversary
love, he takes a shower
as I flip through
the channels
in search of a talk show.

See Notes: 7

In Sickness

To know her is to know
the intimate madness
of a junk drawer;
the madness at the bottom
of a carpetbag —
nail clippers,
old ketchup packets,
loose change,
hard candy hard enough
to chip a front tooth —
Not things as much
As thoughts
is how she described the
rambling sensation.

I know a good man
still in love with his
dementia-suffering wife,
even after she'd hurl insults
from a mouth on fire,
thinking he was
her dead father,
who once dropped
her farm kittens,
one by one,
inside a pillowcase,
tied a tight knot
before casually tossing
the crying, moving bag
into the backyard pond.
Why my kittens, Daddy?!
his wife would scream
While pounding
on her husband's chest
under the glow
of the porch light.

He told me this story
over a beer once —
an old man to a young man,
and in that moment
I knew what I had to do.

See Notes: 8

48

Elephants

To get along
in certain circles
sometimes meant
living with elephants.

The smart ones
carried peanuts
inside their pockets.

I was not one
of the smart ones.

The day I picked up
a brochure
on teaching English
as a second language
from a school
somewhere in Seoul,
was the day I planned
to run from the elephants
for good.

I'd imagined myself
teaching a class
in a room
above a bibimbap cafe,
where afterward I'd go
and drink bubble tea
with new friends.

Then I read about dog
Markets and bosintang -
a popular dog meat soup,
and changed my mind.

Jimmy Russo told me
six months
before he jumped off
the George Washington Bridge
that my problem was
I didn't know myself;
that...and I talked too much.

"Why are you so afraid
Of silence?" Jimmy asked,
before passing me
his cigarette
as we watched the sun
go down
from the Brooklyn Bridge.

Thirty years later,
and I still talk too much,
according to my daughter;
still don't know why
I'm so afraid of silence.

At night, when every sound
is another sound
in the dark,
I think about those elephants;
their big and small gifts.

See Notes: 9

Catherine Jones

Hurt Feelings

Crushed by cruel words
aimed at the heart.
A fragile being already on the cusp
of being swallowed whole.
Hurting like shards of glass
swallowed all the way down
to the soul.

Fragile being never waver
for amongst the clouds
are friendly faces of souls
who have departed.

You are loved and validated.
Even when you feel forgotten
and small
you are worthy and cherished.

Weeping Willow

Weeping willow cries out in tears
Please be kind to my
cascading branches
for they make me
what you see, and why
I am called the weeping willow.

Let my descending branches
lift up as high as possible
for this is when I am
the happiest.
Not when laden down
by my tears.

Tears pushing at my base
Dead remnants, my branches
torn off without regard.
Screams heard with each
branch dropping.
The cries are not audible to
the humans who continue to
prune my being
simply for aesthetic purposes.

I may be more beautiful
to you visually
yet I am destroyed to my core.
Let me weep in my usual silence
while you think I look pleasing.
I know I am only half of what I was
with the departure of
earthward branches
which are older and wiser
and more seasoned than
my new branches.
They may look visually better
but they lack the aged beauty
of their elders.

Perpetual Motion

Eloquent strides in bare feet.
Dress skimming the sand.
Elegant poses.
Essence of natural beauty
exudes from this creature.

Sensuous form.
Wind blowing the dress
into ballooning puffs
like sails on a boat
going with the breeze
naturally flowing.

Swish with each step
of delectable grace.
Each step you take
embellishes a different silhouette

David Blaikie

Midnight Fell on Elizabeth Street

dark freights straining
out from the station
the great slow creaking
of mechanical bones
in the train-track night
boxcars in gathering sway
their mass, a weight so great
it felt as though the earth itself
might crack beneath

and I'd lay there
in my bed, and feel those
cumbrous wheels
and taste the diesel air
and creosote
and see the moonlight fall
a pale hand reaching
through my window
to paint patches on the wall

and I'd think of her
in her beach hut there
on that northern shore
the scent of kelp and sand
her books and pens
and blankets there
and I'd wish to flee
my dim, dark room
and leap upon that train
in all its mighty leaving
and go to her

Slaughterhouse Logs

they'd burst from trucks
when the chain was loosed
dead weight tumbling
sideways
onto bark-stained skids
hulks bleeding balsam
from the chainsaw woods

their criss-cross spill
an avalanche
that could kill a man
with a kick or bounce
or outward swat

as if in final futile rebellion
against the big saw
and their howling
dismemberment
into planks and joists
and two-by-fours
and slab wood junked
for country stoves

trees of a century
sometimes more
lordly spruce
and glimmering pine
shorn of limbs
and seasons
the call of crows
and scattering squirrels

carcasses slashed
in a hail of sawdust
to the chuck and flank
of construction jobs
or the tenderloin cuts
that carpenters prize

then piled in the yard
to bleach like bones
in the lidless noon-day sun

How many elbows to wear out a bar?

I should have asked him
in one of those wet afternoons
when autumn stretched
like a broken train
down the leaf-matted street
and the mood was moth balls
the length of that scarred
old drinkery

he'd have had an answer
of course, though it might
have been anything, leaning back
in that half-tilt way of his
glass and cigarette in hand
spouting another
non-sequitur about the Expos
and the Big O roof
that wouldn't retract
or Hal Banks and his crooks
in the Seamen's Union

or he'd just have
waved a hand and said
How many? How the hell
would I know? I'm working on it.

and he'd have laughed
that flashing blue-eyed laugh
that never failed him
nor let him speak
of the day she died in the fire
and the boy was taken
and the house was lost

though now and then he'd joke
about the night he jumped
from the taxi
and we hauled him back
with mud on his shoes
and the mark that remained
on his forehead

I lost track of him
when he drifted back
to Old Montreal
and missed when he passed
and miss him yet

the big sad cloud that he was
his life a home run
that he never quite hit
a bunch of beers
and what must have
seemed a thousand funerals

David Malone

Aun Aprendo

After Bruce Kauffman's poem "later" from *still arriving*

before these years of canes …
and he now / eighty years on …

Aun aprendo, Goya wrote
on a drawing
he made in his eightieth year –
I'm still learning –
a not too large drawing, in chalk,
of an old, old man,
bearded and robed
(think Moses, in reach of Jericho),
supporting himself
on two solid sticks.

Magnificent is this drawing,
magnificent the strength of its subject;
magnificent the claim he makes for himself.

Even on his deathbed, you suspect,
he was still learning,
as Moses on his deathbed surely was too.

May only I, when that time comes …
May only I ….

The Stream's Source

Though I wasn't lost
I was off the trail.
I wouldn't have been surprised
to see a deer in here, or a moose–
but a horse (though there were farms
not too far by). Barely
was the clearing in which he stood –
the sun now seemingly stalled
in the pit of the sky -
big enough to contain him.

His blackness it couldn't contain,
nor his tears, the source
of the stream that fell away from him,
away from him and down through the stand of young pine
growing up behind.

Because of his distress,
if that's what it was
(though he was trembling as he wept
I couldn't see an injury),
I kept my distance and,
when I spoke,
my voice low.

"Do you want to come with me?
I can get you out."

The tears fell.

Later, I came back.
The sun was moving again
but he was gone –
he and the stream
whose source he'd been.
There wasn't a trace of it.

Silent the pines stood,
green and silent.

Some-Time Gathering Place

Sick and sicker for weeks and weeks –
chemo and radiation at the same time –
I'm just skeletal when,
come the first of November,
finally I get going again.
Short walks to begin,
then a little further,
till about the seventh day
I make it as far as the oak tree in the park down the way,
which is skeletal (as ever) come November too,
and then after that – but never before –
a some-time gathering place
for murders of crows,
whose raucous conversations must,
I think when I hear them from my home,
disturb the furthest skies.
As I rest, skeleton against skeleton,
and wish for a return of strength
I know I'll not have again
(I gasp for breath),
out of the dusk they arrive,
hundreds of them, and light on
the stripped boughs of the tree and me,
as though the tree and I were one;
and as their claws dig into my ghostly flesh,
in that black and awful din
what I feel most is that
I'm grateful to be alive,
even if I've become what I've become,
almost a mockery of what it is to be human.
Though the treatments have stopped, for now,
I'll not beat it. It's in my bones.
So, *please*, I say to the crows,
perhaps a dozen of whom just now call me home,
claw at them if you like, but don't crush them –
not yet – as something else is already doing that.
But if and when I return here again,
and you with your joyous voices aswirl....

Smeared, a little bloody, but elated,
as I make my way back home,
I hear the crows, too, turn and go.

Derek Morley

Sweet Friend

As a flag has symbols
As wind can make it dance
As a rainbow has colors
Beloved friend, so do I have
You
But who are you?
You animate the sunlit hours night lover
You juggle delicate sculptures of clay
Dear, don't let care for carrying carvings
Stop you from
Clearing the fields of your today
And tomorrow multitudes of green shoots
May salute you
For the disciplined generation
Those lost to too much Main St. play
Your hope seeds satiated
By the tears of heart work toiling
That feeling seeking seeing story sharing
Giving life's water
Fields of feed
Nourishment and much needed inquiry
Shine sun into the breach
Through and through
I hope to be there by your side
When the time comes round
To cut open the chocolate soil and reap the rewards
Eat the fruit
On your lips I watch
A story of movement
Inhalation by the hour
Your breathe is sometimes like a slow falling feather
Cycling in a calm and gentle rhythm
Another time your solar plexus claps
A double beat
As your heart rejoices
Then you draw a long, deep invitation to air
Hold it swift and steady
Filling it with an imprint of care
A reflection of some modest joy
It means to you
Something rich in hue
Blood red orange or azure blue

Then in a lingering delivery, softly
Return it to the world
These and many more respirations
are recorded in my memory
Care with air and careful of the enemy
Woman of long dark hair and long deliberations
The quiet moments
between conspiratorial love conversations
I'm impatient to hear again where your waking wills
Always buying one way tickets.
And with a ruse or song you erupt again like a volcano
Rhythm rich, chasing after something far
May you know it when you're near it dear
I trust you know your game
It's in my heart to lay claim
To whatever province we can hope to share
And when the sun sets on that city
That may become the capital of my care
May there be no question of building a Taj there
Upon that ground
Let the stories be written in the shifting earth
Beach papyrus for sand grain hieroglyphics
Bellies full of crystallized laughter
Bejeweled in gems of sitting still
Stalactites of sweet dreams
Realized with some tried some tries
To slow rise spirals
Our wrinkled eyes still holding some surprise
Restful with fulfilled hopes

On a similar dusky night
I once wished I had such a friend
Now with nights bowing head
I sleep with ease again
That's how you push my pen

See Notes: 10

62

Doris Fiszer

Origins

I pocketed starlight before I was born,
roamed the cosmos, explored the surface
of the moon, planned my beginning.

I knew by watching:
the man hovers over the woman,
his talk a warm buzz of love.

The woman arranges his favourite cookies
on a plate, stirs honey into his tea.
They hold hands walking.

I was not yet born but knew,
in this coming life,
I'd shoulder their sufferings.

Do we choose the ones who birth us?

The light I collected shone through them.
I sprinkled moon dust on their bed, my story
as worthy as any other.

Who knows how we arrive, if we carry
fragments of other lives from the blackness
like tiny scars of memory.

See Notes: 11

I linger in the doorway

of my childhood
though I've lost the key.
I linger
in all the other doorways
where I've dwelled.

The pages of the past,
crumpled on the steps,
like a rustle of autumn leaves.

My first bike,
first kiss,
wedding day,
each son's birth,
divorce,
remarriage,
loved ones' deaths,
as easy to recall as morning light
through a kitchen window.

The rest of life's grief and bliss
swirl in a gritty wind.
I'm buried in remembrances —
dreams with slanting floors,
where objects shift and vanish.

See Notes: 12

If I were a river

I'd flow between this world
       and a parallel universe
where my departed dwell.

I'd be greeted by you,
       my loved ones,
splash on shore,
       rest under another sun.

I'd restore your baritone, Father.
       Return with your sky painting, Mother.

The tinkle of voices.

Fragments of their colour-sounds
       float on my waters.

See Notes: 13

Elizabeth Greene

Absence of Dryads

By the time the tree sprawled on my roof
I could see it had no dryad.
Matter without spirit.

The dryad must have vanished bit by bit,
like memory in a shrinking brain.
The leaves had lost their light.

It wasn't tree murder,
like the flowing willow
in our former yard,
comforting guardian,
resting place for birds,
callously cut down.
That dryad must have fled,
her screams inaudible to human ears.

No this was like dementia
where soul recedes,
body remains.
Soul, looking back
from partway to eternity,
must hope that body
will be treated with care,
while body lasts.

This tree, with no dryad,
dead giant, rotten at the core,
cut into chunks,
chopped and chipped —
this rhythmic removal
its only ceremony.
No one mourned.

Ann's Cottage

> Houses have memories.
> Houses hold energies.

By early October, while we were waiting for our tree-damaged house to be repaired, we moved to Ann's cottage. I'd always admired it, a semi-detached old stucco set back from the street behind a lovely double garden with tall trees and a swath of lawn. Its deep blue shutters framed one large twelve-paned window in front, the matching blue door was serene, welcoming but discriminating. I had been as far as the door of Ann's house, seen the dark wood of antiques, glimpsed small peaceful rooms. Ann had also been serene as she glided down our street, often in carefully tailored Indian clothes. Her face was intelligent; her features patrician; her hair still dark. Even walking, she moved to her own music.

One day a few years back, we met in the street. She was agitated (for her). She said she had lost her job with a small publishing company; without it, she couldn't pay her house taxes; she would have to move. Everyone on the street realized what a disaster this was. Ann and her house were so much part of each other. If any of us had been rich, we would have banded together to pay the house taxes, but house taxes are high in our town; we had all we could do to pay our own, especially in the light of constant increases.

Ann's house was on the market for months. "Is it a two-bedroom?" my not-very-sympathetic friend asked. "My father always said, 'Never buy a two-bedroom.'" But maybe the house just didn't want to let Ann go. Houses can be like that. It almost sold, but something went wrong with the survey at the last minute, and. the buyers backed out. Finally, after a year, her neighbours on the other side offered her a low price, taking advantage, we thought, of her age, her singleness, her desperation. She had to accept, but it was humiliating. They offered to buy her antiques, also at a low price. Of course she refused.

It wasn't as if they couldn't have come a little closer to her price. They had four houses, including one on a private island. Ann rented a small house one street over for a while (she told me), then went to live with her daughter in India.

Now, sitting inside Ann's cottage after six weeks of homelessness, I could feel how much it missed her. The floor to ceiling bookcases had a few token magazines and mystery novels and a blanket for the couch. The antiques had been replaced by serviceable generic furniture. The neighbours had turned it into an Air BnB. It wasn't happy. It wanted its own person or people. It wasn't haunted, but it was grieving.

As I sat in her dining/ living room, the heart of the house, I saw traces of Ann—the almost empty bookshelves along the inner wall, probably packed a few short years ago with interesting books, many of them hard-covered, including some she had edited; the good light from the front window in the spacious entrance room and the two side windows that faced the sunrise in this central room which Ann must have enjoyed every morning, the pink-tipped white hydrangeas, vigorous ellipses. I could imagine Ann sitting here reading, having tea, talking with a friend. This house wasn't happy as an Air Bnb.

The house seemed to like us. I think it might have been happy to keep us. But we had our own house, and when the framing repairs started—and finished—suddenly—I was happy to sleep in my own bed, even though there was still a hole in the ceiling. At least I could no longer see sky. And I heard the late October rain on my new roof, grateful that it had waited until the roof was fixed.

We came back to Ann's house in November when our living room and my bedroom were being repaired and painted. The hydrangeas were brown; the trees in front were nearly leafless; the purple Rose of Sharon in the back yard was just a memory, as were the purple perennial geraniums. The house drew into itself preparing for winter. By early December, our ceilings were done; the living room and my bedroom were repainted. We moved back home, only waiting for the flue to be repaired and a new boiler, which was held up until mid-January because of supply chain issues. We borrowed heaters, ran up enormous hydro bills in December and January.

I met Ann's brother in the market and told him I thought the house missed Ann terribly. He said he'd tell her, but when I saw him a few weeks later, he said he thought she couldn't bear to know. She still doesn't walk down our street when she comes back to our town to visit.

Eric Folsom

The Summer of '69

Let there be no moonlight along the beach
Let us navigate for hours, purely
By the sound of surf on our righthand side
And the slight silvering where the waves break.

The next town a glow on the horizon
Our hometown behind us a lesser light.
Past and present are talking together
Like separate voices in a chorus.

In high school, the queers were invisible,
We looked in our mirrors and saw no one.
Nobody resembled us, we were each
Freakishly unique and drenched with shadow.

I don't think any of us heard about
The angry demonstrations at Stonewall
A mere three weeks after graduation.
Even our riots were invisible.

So, who cares about fairies anyways?
Not us in the darkness, no guide but sound
The surging oceans or the raw guitars.
Nothing prevents us from walking forever.

Surely, there's a place by the parking lot
Where a man will ask, do we feel like talking?
"Talk" being a euphemism in this case,
We won't understand more than we do now.

We don't want to talk, we wish to be seen,
We want a world astonished by our wings,
By the stark truth that fairies do exist...
Right beside you, if you could just see us.

Say It (Over and Over Again)

(Homage to Frank Loesser and Jimmy McHugh)

At the end of the call, I added three short words
To say without saying, how I missed being close,
Joked briefly about notional proclivities
And our formerly mutual activities,
All the more improbable in pandemic times,
Desires tossed off in a coded expression
Awkward and anodyne, an amateur helpline
Not a phrase that could really make us feel sublime.

To travel the continent on planes that don't fly
Just to greet you with your mask on six feet away
Is more than absurd, so let microwaves haul words
Across the sky, an owl's wing through dark forest.

Dear friend, tune your heart to the soundscape of the night,
Who loves who over and over beneath starlight.

You Don't Know What Love Is

(Homage to Don Raye and Gene De Paul)

No one's born understanding the love of others
At first, we simply notice who offers us care,
Creating attachments with people who are kind
Our fortunate hearts finetuning a laggard mind.

We swallow harsh lessons once goodbye is for good
Gather skills for staying, when we think we should,
Subtracted, love retains something residual
Of more value than just one individual.

Empty beds grow bigger, our dream selves grow humble
Our lips, deprived of kisses, feel less kissable,
The habit of persistence becomes a stale joke
We shiver inside memory's ill-fitting cloak.

The truth unlearned, which we struggle to discover
Is what being loved might feel like for our lover.

Gwenith M Whitford

The Wisdom of Trees

Deciduous and Coniferous Trees
Offer us their gifts:
Autumn splendor and evergreen delight
Bearing sustenance: nuts, fruit, sap and seeds
Offering shade under their canopy
A haven for birds and other beings
Beauty in abundance
In every season.

Their absorption of CO_2
Allows us to breathe more easily.
Yet we don't hesitate
To take more than we need
Harvesting for avarice and prosperity
Destroying 'mother trees' needlessly
As the temperature climbs higher
Wiping out forests with devastating fires.

Despite this careless destruction,
We now know
That trees extend their roots outward,
Forging symbiotic relationships,
holding the soil in place
With their collective strength.
They bond to keep the earth alive:
It is they that are wise.

Summer Cold

Heavy, humid, sultry days
Streaming sweat; lethargy prevails.

Sweltering heat bounces off concrete
No reprieve without a/c
Until darkening days and barren trees
Usher in the season of bleak.

Its dreary, freezing, constant chill
Segues into the coldest months
When dreams defy logic
With escapes to tropical climes
Where a taste of insufferable summer
Is deemed perfectly fine.

Mountain Majesty

Diablotin* is smiling today.
Finally -
a fair-weather sign.
I've been waiting
a while
to see Her shrouded face
and all its imperfections
uncovered,
revealing
Her verdant beauty.
From a distance,
across ridges and valleys
I note shape,
structure
and surface,
standing tall
above all:
at 4 7 4 7, the Pride
of Dominica,
scarred by storms
marred by barren spaces
sheltered
by resilient canopy,
montane forest
and elfin woodlands,
renewed
over centuries.
In bright morning light
cloud cover removed,
She is our Majesty,
a Dominican monument,
for true.

*See Notes: 14

Honey Novick

Oh, Mother Earth (song lyrics)

words and music: Honey Novick

CHORUS:
> *Oh, mother earth, we are your children*
> *trees'n'people'n'field'n'stream*
> *Oh, mother earth, we are your children*
> *we want to thank you, we want to dream*

Expediency lives in our hearts, just for a dollar,
    just for a buck
We rip off tomorrow, we sell off today
What makes us think we won't have to pay?

> *CHORUS*

The trees give their lives to unmask people's greed
People and trees are all family
We're killing this planet by selling our mother

> *CHORUS*

How can I be still and keep my mouth shut?
The air is polluted, the water is too.
Our time may be borrowed, our time may be through
We're selling our future by hating our mother

> *CHORUS*

My cry is a warning the chaos is near,
We're killing our planet by bowing to fear
Can you hear me Mother Earth?
The love in my heart?
My laughter is hidden, my tears everflow

> *CHORUS*

Our hearts they are breaking and need to fulfilled
This planet is family it mustn't be killed

FINAL CHORUS
> *Oh, Mother Earth, We are your children*
> *Trees'n'people'n'field'n'stream*
> *Oh, Mother Earth, We are your children*
> *We NEED to thank you, we NEED to dream.*

See Notes: 15

J. Edgar*

Part 1

"J. Edgar"*, a movie, was on TV at the time of this writing
I couldn't watch it
It reminded me of a time my parents took into our home
a family of 4 (husband, wife, son and daughter)
not because they were communists (they were)
            but because they were Jews.
The husband was imprisoned for his beliefs
Upon release, they were homeless but not for long
and thus my life changed (for the better).
These wonderful people were humanistic, caring
            and never lost a sense of purpose
They didn't demean a child (me)
didn't disrespect the differing opinions of my father
who really didn't want them but bowed to the demands
            of what things cost
and so their rent money was necessary.
And now I'm reminded of those days
the days when I would peak out the window and see men
sitting in a sedan outside our house
day after day
when I asked my mother about this, she said
"get away from the window and don't move the curtain"
this is in my life, I'm too young to know
            about Nazi Germany and WWII but
I clearly remember McCarthyism in CANADA,
            I repeat in Canada!!!
red-baiting

I fear we've gone back in time to the early 1950 years
when it was prudent to get away from the window and
            not move the curtains
I thought we came a long way, baby
I thought the war was worth fighting for and it was
at least fighting Nazis in WWII was and always will be
and now we're back there again
a reporter ordered from her job by a nation's president
a federal judge fired for forewarning the same president
he who offered to bring jobs back
Huh!!!
if you can't muzzle them, get rid of them
if they look too ugly put them somewhere they can't be seen

if they can't fight and put their lives on the line,
        they become invisible
these are the times
cynical, yes
hopeless, not

Part 2

In the 2010s, I was artist in residence for a theatre company
to help out, I did box office one Friday evening
I was looking down at the till
when I looked up, a face stared at me
I was dazed, like a deer in headlights
the face was the same face as the boy in the family that lived
with us in the 1950s
I said, "are your grandparents Bella and Joe?"
"Yes," she replied, "how did you know?"
I said, "You have Arthur's face"
I wanted to keep in touch with her
after several years, we connected
today we drove together, here, to the Kingston Arts Festival.
A spiritual thread, a true connection is never broken.

*See Notes: 16
See Notes: 17

Jane Macdonald

Mr. Nyman's Dutch Garden

Tulips, all of them the same gormless yellow
and in-your-face red, ornament the front yard
of every house on his street, an onslaught,
issuing yearly from the card table in his driveway
where he set out paper bags of bulbs.
They conquered the neighbourhood.
He died, Mr. Nyman, but last spring
after a lifetime of Aprils I took him up
on the invitation he'd planted by the walkway:
Open Garden. Come In.
His funeral was in November and the sign's been
uprooted, but today, if I slow past the house,
I catch sight of his tulips marching the length
of his back garden to the millpond,
swerving aflame around knots of crazy narcissi
still nodding at their reflections.
Mr. Nyman invited everyone
to lose themselves awhile
in that categorical beauty.
But that's not why I stopped.
Humiliated by all my little losses,
how other people's lives are better than mine,
I swear I did not mean to overlook
how the plum blossom flares on its bare dumb branch,
or how the magnolia tree in his side yard
crushes the new grass with its grape soda petals.

In Memoriam

Surprising this fog, damp
on my face and hands
as I pedal over to the post office.

I've 3 letters to mail, in thanks
for cards the recipients sent us
of sympathy.

November is the month the veil thins.
Hands gripping the handlebar, my long bones
pumping the wheel, I could be a skeleton

The toddler chased by its mom in the park,
clothed in black,
will grow up

Each person I meet in the street
I need to tell them: She's gone.
Our girl, become a young woman and gone.

But I know, I know each of us
bears our dead. On Saturday past
while we cleared the plates at the reception,

a boy on his dirt bike
dies in a crash. On Sunday they planted a post,
hung a single tire, 3 of his friends,

their cheeks reddened in the flaring autumn light,
flanked by vehicles their parents pulled onto the verge
to let them out to dig.

Oh that our hearts should crack and not break.
Death inside life, life inside death,
each of us walking the ground as through mist.

That we should walk together.

See Notes: 18

Two Years ago a Trumpeter Swan was Frozen in the Harbour

Open water today, still and grey. The sky to the north
is white as the fields, thundering blue to the south,
like horses stampeding.
My neighbour's car when I return
is not in front of her house. She's left
her Christmas lights on, in daylight,
around the porch, and on the tree in the front room.
It's a small house, the living room
only big enough for a hospital bed, her mother in it
two months, delicate breath, bones of a sparrow.

I used to think pines trees in gardens cheerless.
One stands guard where we live now,
and from my bedroom on the second floor I can see
it's weighted with cones. Lemon trees also bear
heavy fruit even as new blossoms come on.
I don't expect I'll have another garden
or a lemon tree as I did in California.

This afternoon in sudden snow I fixed my eyes
on one flake, followed its descent
past the hood of my car.
Long ago, home to Red Deer from Lethbridge, my father
fell asleep at the wheel. I imagine
there were no pines for miles,
but there would have been cottonwoods.
Their downy fluff fills the sky when they seed,
like snow in summer, thick as forgetting.
It was September when he died. Their leaves
would be yellowing around then –
yellow hearts and the blue sky behind them –
which he wouldn't have seen as he crashed, it was night,
the sun on the other side of the world.

See Notes: 19

80

Jason Heroux

from **From There, the Visitor***

Sounds. Why are they here, and where do they come from? Everything we hear is a sound made by something in this world, with one exception. Silence. Silence is rooted where it is, and cannot be generated, only found. It took 150 million years for the silence in the Drogarati Cave to develop into what it is today. When we hear silence in the modern world we feel connected to a deeper sense of time and being. We sense an abundant restoration of ancient energy. For all intents and purposes silence is always home. Sounds, on the other hand, have no home. They are always passing through, moving forward. A sound can't go back to where it was from. It flees its birthplace in the hopes of reaching a place where it can be heard. Perhaps a healthy world is one full of new, diverse sounds that belong where they are. Perhaps every noise needs our help. Sounds are like visitors, seeking refuge. And how we welcome them, or block them out, informs how we engage with our world.

"Drogarati Cave consists of two parts. The part accessible to tourists consists of a long corridor that leads to the Royal Balcony, a natural platform of stalactites that beautifully reflect the light. From there, the visitor can see the Chamber of Exaltation, which has great acoustics."

From "greeka.com/ionian/kefalonia/sightseeing/kefalonia-drogarati-cave"

Sounds can't return to where they originated from. They have no family to return to. Wherever it's heard, a sound is home.

Some sounds arrive vibrant and full of life, abundant, bountiful, other sounds arrive weak, barely alive, growing quieter.

What forces a sound to flee its own country? Why do we hear so many sounds from elsewhere?

Countless sounds have died on their way to being heard, and there is nowhere in the world to bury them, no way to scatter their cremated ashes.

An unheard sound has no final resting place, and quite a few are so young, they need time to grow, time to make a sound of their own. Many sounds change how they sound hoping to belong.

*See Notes: 20

Jen Frankel

Strays

(Menopause Press, poem of the month 2017)

I don't bring home strays
I said to the baby bird
On its side on the side-
Walk
I know life +
I know death +
Their delicate, remorseless interplay
I know it may be more cruel
To pluck a stray from the street
Than to allow life +
Death to have their way

I don't bring home strays
I said to the man
The look in his eyes not
Too unlike that of the baby bird
I know love +
I know emptiness +
Their siren-urgent sway
The cost to use the semblance of one
To fill the other
I have heard
Every reason in the book
For you to stay –
And so I repeat
I don't take home strays

Let death have its way
Let love last a day
'Til emptiness returns to play
But life, sweet life

Is not afraid

Therapy

Loving you is just like being in therapy
I'm with you an hour and then you want me to leave
I pay more for it than I can afford
I'm still unsatisfied when you show me the door

Out of Despair Comes Life

Over the hill shall we say
It's a lonely place of good intentions shelved
Ambitions questioned
Can I really
Is it gone
Am I all but done

I sit to journal all my flaws
My failings my heartache my loss
The dreams that never fled
Although they stubbornly refuse to come true
All those endless days of prodding at the walls
Searching for the way forward
Digging test bore holes in the ground
Finding nothing but sand in the sample cores
Knowing that the woman just feet away has again struck gold
It can go far to make this woman bitter

And resentful of her own bitterness
When there can be joy if only she stops looking in
And instead puts it all out there
Down
On the page
Where it's suddenly manageable
And more
Where it changes into something not just ready to be handled
But a gift
An inspiration to subsume grief and regret
In creative thought and new beginnings

Wait for peace at your peril
Serenity comes in movement
In restless thought and open mind
In the words on the page
And the comfort they bring

Jennifer Londry

Project City

Octogenarian grips two trekking poles.
Goose down navy pea coat tightly fastened at the neck,
a black cap tugged over deaf aids masks the echo
of his blue veined lonesome
that creaks in his ears like a rusty hinge

on a saloon door in a ghost town
that hasn't seen a patron in years.

Queen Street

Under her black umbrella, a robin's-egg-blue
long sleeve shirt,
yellow pants, fishing-shack-green socks,
and browns loafers.

Leash wrapped around her wrist is tethered
to a dog.
Fur the colour of spun gold.

Sidewalk is crematorium.
A continuous halo of heat that hovers
like a mirage around dog and its owner vanishing.

Jennifer Verardi

The Shape of Fire

My body was tired and happiness was fleeting.
All of my power was held in that single moment,
And then it was crushed into a million pieces.
And I watched it burst into flames.

My entire world changed, lost its meaning.
My heart beat hard in my chest – trying to break it.
Then all of my dreams became rearranged…
Shaped my grief into burning red flames;
I'd scream trying to spark light with a broken match,
Watching my uncontrollable ocean of grief spill out.
It mistook my happiness for a game,
And misused my sorrow to attach,
Waiting for the next helpful sound.
Here, though, is where I built the first door,
and my castle walls of dangerous flames,
To protect this house of fire.

There is where I lay in my shadow,
trying to remember that I am stronger than the pain,
while I watch every single fire spiral.
As tired eyes became too heavy,
To keep up with this stream of memories,
My mind struggled to connect any dots.

Here is where I remember that,
You can change the shape of fiery things,
but not how you fought through them.

All Roads Lead Home

Beginning to wake up all of the bones
Deep within the dead of cold
Buried under all of the stones
That were thrown from golden thrones
Laying out all of your bones
Underneath the sky
All on your own
Hum your song of sweet hopeful prose

Dig into the unknown – All roads lead home
Don't fear being alone – All roads lead home
Your journey is your own

Waking up all the noise
Locked inside of your achy joints
Build that heat up to destroy
The fear that guides you to avoid
Gotta learn how to speak your voice
And don't be afraid to make a choice

Dig into the unknown– All roads lead home
Don't fear if you're alone – All roads lead home
You get to choose which way you roam

Waking up all the truths
Name the world as it has named you
You crack the riddle and then you solve the proof
Each time you fail you cut your tooth
All of your mistakes grow you up from your youth
As you wake up all of those sleeping bones
And you lay them out all on your own
Building you up stronger than ever before
Did you know that you grew, each time it tore

Dig into the unknown – All roads lead home
Embrace the fear when you're alone
You get to choose the way you go

Dig into the unknown– All roads lead home
Embrace the fear when you're alone – All roads lead home
Don't you fear bein' alone Because all roads lead home

Blurry and Beautiful

Livin' in puzzles felt easier for the longest time
Livin' obscure double meanings and running breathless
The anxiety felt normal to hold,
Like a tiny globe made of glass,
You ran too fast, and it felt and it broke

You've been running through so many hoops– I know
Sometimes it feels like you've got nothing left
But when it doesn't go right – you've Gotta pull left

The beauty is in the attempt,
And, now you get to choose your next dream

This journey is a mystery, but you're still graceful
It might feel ordinary, but believe that it's magical
It's Okay when it looks blurry
Cause it's still beautiful

Sorting through innocence and experience
Full of delicate views and staggering truths
Where disjointed memories and mixed metaphors
Marry half truths to your tender core

Pressed against fire and it almost burned you down
You rose from the ashes– even without a crown
Look at your hands how they learn to reach, grip, And, let go
The beauty is in how you grew
And, now you get to choose your next dream

This journey is a mystery, but you're still graceful
It might feel ordinary, but believe that it's magical
It's Okay when it looks blurry
It's still beautiful

The world is living in a weak time of peace
Don't know who to trust, and some aren't free
They speak damned rhymes that break ties like razors
To even a lion heart

But they've miscalculated and misjudged
Emotional intelligence and empathy for fragility
The outcast state is only temporary
Don't let them bury your fire underneath their dirt

The beauty is in how you see,
And, now you get to choose your next dream

Joel Giroux

Lily in the Hosta
  for my father

I saw a long fury of hosta in the grass
when I walked past my neighbour's garden.
It stretched the lawn beside their house
to give up a blast of bright leaves

ringed with forest green. Inside that glorious
mess, verdant and flush, a lily emerged
like a white hand in bloom, offering
a grace unlike anything else that corner plot

had ever given before, or ever will again.
A floral glance bright as new life,
as living itself, until gone for the season,
world's end, a whirl of white distended

and slight, but righteous, and alive, alive still —

Last Word

Your last word still whooping inside,
you wake to find your wings gone;
some will say you only dreamed them.
Your arms hold hands behind your head
instead, a blooming of bright flowers
in someone else's midnight garden.

Your last word stopped up inside,
you pray a hand pokes free of the wall
with a note you yourself wrote just now,
in a dream: *if your last word swoons,*
then you'd better start singing,
even if you're only alone with the moon
shining down to listen.

Your last word stuck in your teeth,
you clear your throat to sing
despite everything; coughing, sitting
on the cliff of your bed with the ghosts
you unwittingly called up like a ring
of yawning clouds you hope can hold off
blinding day, mocked nightly
      by the moon
          who now throws
      her blue shadow
          over everything
to hear you finally sing:
an appeal little more
      than bluish silence, much less
          than just a whoosh in space:
      a lingering wish

          in a pile of notes
      set fire by the bright
light of your flickering
      tongue, its lunatic
          clicks, and its divine,
      devoted stuttering.

The Retail Playlist

The retail playlist hums along with constant
nostalgia for a life you sometimes wish
you'd long forgotten, but can't shake off
because the tuneage they keep piping
through tinny speakers that hang above us like
remote drones frighteningly still throughout
the store keep dripping down a music light
and dry as dust. There are aisles full of product
covered in a flimsy sheen of musical notes
discarded by the air, bits of song that float
down throughout the business day,
settling on coffee makers, lawnmowers,
scented candles, cast iron pans always
on sale. Toasters, impact drills,
fishing tackle, bungee cords, chocolate bars,
disposable pens — all wear the invisible
quilt of what were once piquant sharps
and flats, played now only by rote,
rattling with the memories they keep holed up
inside them, tiny drawers of sound opening
and closing all the business day long,
halted now and then by digital bird squawk
from Employee Facing Devices that go off
in our pockets like sonic glitter bombs
for e-comm orders or curbside pickups or warehouse calls:
Warehouse? Pause. *Warehouse here.* Pause again.
Can you find product number 107– 8009
times two for a gentleman in aisle 43 with
the adorable blue tick hound on a pink leash?
Who knows what smidgen of inventory belongs
to those numbers any more than we know
how hazy memories fasten to swirling tones,
those sloughed off flakes of sound that float down,
settle on shelves in the aisles, or tangle the hairs
on our arms, which stand up shocked at old emotions
we suddenly believe might be lurking somewhere
on the floor, or in warehouse, still waiting for our hands
to pluck them from their fading places, a fallen music
to quietly deflate time and space, to sound
only loud enough to sigh, round
the air, then stop, and disappear.

Judith Popiel

Summer: The Great Oak Canopy

Rich layers of colourfully green and
brown shaped Oak leaves
adorn your branches

Pressing their silent, soothing
healing natural beauty against
my unworthy consciousness.

Standing silently
statuesque like
upon green grass
growing beneath your trunk
glancing upward
your magnificent beauty
speaks to my subconscious
outstretched tentacles of gnarled branches
a backdrop
against the blue blue sky above
seem to speak of your ageless
grace and years of definition

Heart surrenders to your
overwhelming beauty
unnecessary and frivolous
stirrings of the mind
overshadow this temporary moment
of bliss.

Conscious feelings of pure natural
grace wrap themselves around me
seeping into my bosom
these archetypal oaks
bringing a consciousness permeating
beneath the skin into those deeper
layers beyond time and space
where memories are held in tact

Nourishment for the soul
on a more cloudy day.

Oak Forest Before Winter Solstice

Tall and straight your many trunks stand
Roots buried deep beneath carpet of
fallen leaves
Your sturdy trunk holding leftover
expanding branches
Silhouetted against cold dreary atmosphere
of an almost winter like day
Weary from adorning us from summers
splendour
Your branches hold piercing silence
of the moment
It's as if the fall weather has shaved your
branches razor thin
Brought you to the core of your beauty
Standing momentarily in awe
Silence of Equinox more profound
No wind
Just a sacred stillness
Amongst your dormant trunk
Squirrels chirping in the distance
As if singing the swan song of summer
Naked you are
Before my very eyes
Sacred stillness emerges within mind
Warns my challenged body
Of coming Winter months
Glory of summer
Your great indelible canopy
Not lost
Just dormant in my consciousness
Observing and listening attentively
Against the mist of the mind
Remembering the spectacle of Summer
And what lay beneath the surface
Winter Solstice brings new horizons
More light
More insight into the natural world
of this Oak Forest

Flocks of Canadian Geese fly overhead
Their distinct distant cries
Heard every year
Overshadow the contemplative silence
of the moment.

Standing still
Amongst these great oaks
I await the Equinox
Savouring Winter's blessings.

Kate Marshall Flaherty

Poplar Grove
for R.F.

After many years, my first love took me
to his favourite poplar grove.
Mist and drizzle
made coins of autumn leaves,
gold against grey sky. The hush
and breath of trees made me listen.

I know now
inosculation is the means a tree has
of growing through a fence.
While its deep-digging filaments
search through subsoil, its noble limbs
are slow and patient
as they feel around the chain-link metal,
surround it, overcome
their obstacle with spring buds.

It takes many year-rings to see this —
time in tree language is slow
as sap before thaw.

I hold a space of tree-secrets;
cool wet air in my lungs,
my ribs expanding
to exhale gratitude.
In the autumn I attend to the poplars
nourishing each other,
their shimmering leaves
settling on soggy ground
to feed the next generation.

See Notes: 21

Sel

*"I would never scold an onion
for causing tears"*
       Naomi Shihab Nye

I learned
the salt content of tears
is the same as blood
and the sea—

that lysosomes
are healing enzymes,

and sea salt
has nourishing minerals.

We are the same three-fourths water
as the earth.

Grey Dead Sea salt is the same
as pinkish Himalayan;

both, so far from home.

Tears are the same saline
whether they fall to the ground
unnoticed,
or streak cheeks pressed close
in a refugee boat. They dissolve
the borders, or should.

Let us not wait
for another boy washed up on shore.

Earth mother, salt sister, sanguine Sophia,
this planet needs our water-wisdom.

Salt, enzyme, saline, suffering—
let fear dissolve
into the 73% that is us all.

See Notes: 22

White on Green

Out my window this morning, green
leaves speckled with something—
bits of cry-crust, crumbs of sleep choke stomas,
                    dried tree tears—
it makes me sad to see this
leeching white on green, parched dust from ducts
clogging leafy vein lines,

                    speckled confetti of mourning,
confectioner's dusting where it shouldn't
be—not sweet, but acid–
bitter reminder of rain, what we have done
to our home.

                    Willows weep and dry-bend,
oaks host moth-nests crawling with eaters,
mighty maples droop, pocked
with unnatural spots—a plague of arbor leprosy,

pox hurting heartwood, marks
under a yellow haze of summer grit and gas
suffocate our siblings who purify air.

                    Lung to lung, I wheeze out
my thanks, wonder what can I do, how
can leaf rot be cured
of this bleached-as-sterile-gauze, killer?

Let my prayer float up, not so simple
as to *say the word and be healed.*
I see a glut
of caterpillars gorging,
        cocooning—
                emerging
                        wet winged
        into a new juice—

Is this us?

See Notes: 23

Kelsey Newman Reed

golden hour

in the golden hour
when the sun sets
across the water
the trees tremor
in the loss of light
swaying to the moons
embrace

i reflect on the day
how the leaves made
shadows across the walls
how another day is lost
in a sea of memories

empty swing set

the empty swing set rustles in the breeze
where the trees used to be–
still, are,
but far away
in my mind that plays tricks
on how i see

i remember the shape of the leaves
the shape of you
as you swung too fast
with your back to me

in my mind that plays tricks:

it still sees you on the empty swing set
still feels how the breeze rustled my hair
still feels how it felt to be near you
where the trees used to be–
still, are,

but far away

what we find

the lavender bits
                    collect ' " ' ' "
instead of dust

&& in between
our hands match / \ meet there
to hold still
            what flutters ~ ~

like magic
like rocks
like strength

we find in
            = here =

Leslie Saunders

What's Your Favourite...?

I confess it's not a game I like

if pressed, I might tell you a book
that's hit my all-time top 100 list
or a must-play piece of music
but to pick– oh say – my preferred
breed of horse
from that catalogue of pure nobility – no.

but I can, with absolute, 100 percent certainty,
tell you the best hug

it was that day

shortly after my son died,
and I'm on the lawn
picking up after the dog
when up the street comes Chuck
ripe in the aroma of his morning run

opens his arms, says, "oh Leslie"
pulls enfolds me long and tight

while the drip of his sticky sweat,
plip-plops into the dip of my collar bone,
and the pendulum swing of the poop-bag
dangling from my hand
knocks   again and again   against him

This Small Thing

sliding the soft white sock
over the pudgy pink appeal
of my baby brother's toes

slipping it seamless as cream round
the mound of his heel and onto
the button bones
of his little ankle, I couldn't
and wouldn't stop myself

couldn't and wouldn't not

percuss my playful fingers
up and down
his silky soles
say

*"tickle feeties number one, and
tickle feeties number two"*

before pressing
each plump perfect package
into its shoe

Watching You Tube

Ballet   a beautiful piece,
the costumes perfect,
muted browns and grays, portraying peasants

and each danseuse explained
in their separate way
what we mean by a word like 'grace'
the choreography complex, yet full of play
the bodies strong, their faces calm,
deeply intent
but if you look closely, you'll see
that most of them
have an intellectual disability

but should we?
look closely?

or is the truer view
simple:
they are dancers

Louise Carson

Scattershot and arrow

First storm of the season.
Counting forward – four more months.
Thirty or more poems, perhaps.
Perhaps a book – *the* book.

Like *the* poem.
If you aim well enough –
or is it, if you randomly shoot enough –
you're bound to hit your mark.

It's funny, but – success or failure –
it feels the same at the time. Like love.
The fun is in the making.
Scattershot *or* arrow.

When poets die

for Pat Lane, Mary Oliver and W. S. Merwin

When poets die and you stand at the sink,
scrubbing last night's soup pot –

Before their reputations are stuffed and mounted,
their words selected, collected –
as you repot and water orchids –

One flower spike, supposed to grow
out between two stiff leaves,
has got itself caught,
is looping back
in to the central stalk,

there to open
small secret flowers
in that dark.

The last thing

What's the last thing that made me cry?
Last night's retirement of Bob Cole –
hockey announcer for most of my life –
eighty-five, the age my dad would be if he –

Or a father's face – his son one
of the Humboldt Broncos –
on the one-year anniversary.
A father's face, saying how proud –

Or this morning's poem, in which
a convergence of women who helped each other
survive Bergen-Belsen,
meet three lifetimes later and can smile.

Loss, pity, joy. I guess
I could ask you: what was your
last thing? Moss?
A city? A toy?

Madison Cuddon

Fallen

Hardened are the eyes of an angel fallen-
Stoney are the eyes of one who bears the scars
but never the fall.
Twisting and turning, you maniacal shapeshifter
you tempt me-
with worn blends of
feelings
With truths

You understand my desires by no empathy of your own.
This apple is ripe-
the Serpent to my Eve.
I am draining into you now-
my time, my lessons,
my life force.
As much my fault as your flaws.

With me, you steal regret and replace it with regency.
I long to understand your thoughts,
how you scheme your dreams.
How can you place love in my palms
but still tell me nothing is there,
simply because you'd forgotten where you placed it?
In between salt-stained sobs,
laughter bounces off walls.
Indomitable fallen angel-
distance could never affect influence.

A Sense of Self

Isolation– pure and sweet.
What will I do when the haunting spirit
of my quiet mind finds me once again?
I was too philosophical in my childhood.
Harsh realities were too common to be ignored.
Maybe to be introspective when you're young is
to abandon that very youth.

I'd speak to myself, the only one who'd understand.
And realize that self-destruction has
a kind of unexplainable opulence to it.

The open window of my bedroom
lets in the harsh winter wind,
And the unlocked doors release hell into my space.
"Oh, sweet girl, you don't deserve this."
A voice– my saviour,
I shiver in their arms.
Dreams like these come and go-
Bud oddly, my hero and my villain wear the same face.

Isn't it freeing when you abandon your need to
disguise your sickening self-awareness?

The Food of Love

Dancing– bodies rushing together, hearts beating.
Breath heavy with passion,
so physical and mesmerizing it
now turns to carnage in my hands.
Do you want more?

I could strip the very meat off my bones
to feed your hunger–
Despite your disgust I'd beg you to take it
"Satisfy yourself."

I'd love to be a mother, if you'd let me be your wife.
The house is painted white, the doorway made of fire.
Children laughing in the backyard,
Dancing in the breeze
Snow is falling into our outstretched palms,
melts on our smiles,
Snow– from painting grey skies blue.

You are out for blood but I've already been sucked dry

Maria Mitea

excarnation

with white gloves
he carries it on his shoulders, – the sand
shatters–
–in the dance of the heat

the eagles wait solemnly

leave my body soft
in the air, leave it up
up
on the tower of silence
at the origin of rain

forbidden to the earth
waiting for the rescuers of the sky

yugen

it's enough to breathe
to touch you

it's enough to breathe
let your voice sing

it's enough to breathe
to see you come and go
walk like an angel

I am The Wind

Crying
Curbing
Breaking
Branches

Passing storm
Leaving silent
Bending
Hitting darkness
In your windows

I can sing
I can cry

I can sing a lullaby
Howl like a wolf
I can shake up dreamers in the dark

I am the wind

The crying
The breaking
The singing
The barking

I am the terror of dry branches

Meg Freer

Pitch-Perfect Dreams

summer ease, think breeze
I'll simply notice, but not name it

quick as a splinter, I slip a ball
of tangerine-light between my ribs

tighten my eyebrows, look straight ahead
with bright eyes, inhale pale yellow

from the edges of sunset
to fill constricted spaces

an opportunity to pause and regret
reflect on a smooth flow of water

that spins out of control
chaos that kisses with purpose

See Notes: 24

Seeds of Control

The daisy I pick from the hoarder's overgrown yard
at 11:00 p.m. lasts a week in a glass of water,
the daisy from my lawn barely a day.

The wrecking yard across town, testimony to loss
of control, sports a few seasonal additions
amid goldenrod and chicory—jet ski, dune buggy,
one small egg-shaped camper trailer.

Midsummer, the garden cosmos becomes unruly,
waving shades of pink in a glorious free-for-all,
each single bloom a simple cartoon flower.

Late in August, one feeble sunflower
emerges from seeds I planted by the garage.
Down the street, a healthy stand of them bursts
from the hoarder's weeds, as if to taunt me.

See Notes: 25

Interwoven

A lost hen walked down
our city driveway this morning,
headed for a better spot
in the pecking order, or perhaps
someone's evening soup.

The drumbeat in the song
on the car radio sounded
exactly like the turn signal,
or the hen's tapping feet,
and I tried in vain to turn it off.

I received news of my mother:
"The toe that was bothering her
has been taken care of. When your feet
hurt, you hurt all over, so now she will
stand and sleep in comfort: Huzzah!"

When my daughter was young,
she used to write things on small
pieces of paper, random phrases
such as: *ask the corn foot club*
or: *the boot cracks in sore fury.*

Take me on a tour of the generations,
weave straight lines into curves, let me feel
the ache of evolution. Where words
leave off, what begins? My hands feel
the motions, braid invisible hair.

See Notes: 26

Mike Madill

Already Full

Mother says hello without
so much as a glance, tossing lettuce
in a metal colander over the sink,
each shake of her double-fisted grip
sending more shreds skywards.

Dad's to my right at the table,
his one eye trickling despite his praise
for the new prescription. My brother
Steve, their trusted master of the grill,
lords over the table: *Did you know
Mars has nine separate moons?*

The potato salad is riddled with sharp
slivers of radish; a grass-coloured knoll
of alien pickles conspire their hostile
take-over of my plate. I try to put off
the inevitable, stare out the picture window
at the pasture beyond, half a dozen
Holsteins jostling at the fence, staring back.

The gossip Mother let slip once about
Steve's girl in Rochester won't be
spoken of today. Next time I'm here
will be Christmas, small talk still
in the way, silences stuck together
like bread and butter far beyond
their best before dates.

Fraying

If I were to exhume my teddy-bear
from storage, would he still
recognize me? I recall the winter
my grandmother made him
a new coat head-to-toe, even
his steadfast, amber eyes
buried under a newly-knit face.
I was never convinced
he remained inside, or saw me
as clearly after that, but we made do.

My own fraying can't be concealed
half as neatly. I worry one day
I'll walk into a mirror, only to find
splinters of me – jagged, spotty and dull.
Would it come as a shock,
or simply be grim confirmation
that the impression I make has finally
ebbed beyond the ether's edge?

I could pretend to embrace
my new-found rendering like a
mummified toy bear, but
where's the comfort in that?
Pass a hundred souls on the street
saddled with their own growing
translucence, dissolving bucket lists:
a perfect cookbook recipe
to see I'm no more doomed
than everyone else.

Verdicts

More than an hour ago,
an orderly in merlot-coloured scrubs
took you away for good
news or bad, your gait tense,
receding. You dressed all in black
for the follow-up –
the reaper and the chosen
all rolled into one.
Left behind in an isolated corner
of Neurology's waiting room,
my only witness a plastic peace lily
in fake wicker, mute as
an afternoon moon.
The rumbling city's discontent
shivers the surface within
my half-empty bottle of Evian.
A flat-screen tv looms
high on its wall, nattering on
about the day's unfolding, stories
tumbling down into indifference
amid sagging overcoats, shouldered
knapsacks, purse straps cinched tight.
Stares stuck to the floor, overdue
verdicts consigned to silent, obedient
rows. Squealing doors down the hall,
wheezing elevator chimes, relentless
churning of the heating vents.
The haunting up-and-down strains
of hushed chatter
nursed at the front desk.

Nathalie Sorensen

High Summer, Eastern Ontario

On a country road, fully leafed trees
arch over worn gravel
a cloister of green shade
pierced by glints of sun,
on buttercups, grasses, Queen Anne's Lace.

A solitary house, white clapboard,
green door and shutters,
sits well back of the road,
bordered by purple iris,
pink and white peonies.

A checked cloth, red and blue,
covers a small table set by the side of the road.
On it is a bowl of sugar snap-peas,
a stack of homemade fruit pies neatly boxed,
a small scale to weigh purchases, a can for money,
and a sign listing prices: peas, $5.00 per half kg,
pies: raspberry, strawberry, apple, $10.00.

No one is about in the quiet,
just a chipmunk scurrying,
just bees on peonies, a robin calling,
two yellow swallowtails on white lace,
and the table unattended.

Lilwen's Last Years

Work done, family grown,
Lilwen and Calum retire to the woods,
a small sunny room, a table piled with books.

Lilwen seldom stirs from home
all errands left to Calum.
She gazes at a green meadow
birch trees, spring daffodils,
goldfinch and nuthatch feeding.
Once a gray wolf appears,
their dog barking madly.
Who needs town? she says.

Near the end their world shrinks again
– a small suite in a retirement home,
neighbours who do not read.

Only the owner, a Russian émigré,
interests Lilwen.
Her study shifts to Russian history,
politics, literature. Her mind roams
long reaches of the steppes,
the reign of Catherine the Great,
her reforms, her palaces, her lovers,
the murders of Czar Nicholas
and all his family, Tolstoy wearing
the shirts of serfs in his last years.

Lilwen recalls with fondness
her tidy cottage.
Her home now is the sweep
of Russia's lonely landscapes.
In her last days she breathes
the fresh wind of the steppes.
It feels like the future.

Glyph of Time
(for a perfect mollusk fossil)

In a young earth full of juice
you swirled in shimmering surf,
sweeping in and out, froth of warm seas
on your glistening shell
as you fell beyond the tide.

Slowly your life expired: silt drifted
across your delicate flutes
closed over your quivering body
until, at last, you lay beneath
the surface of the lively world.

The world went on.
Fish swam ashore
dinosaurs grew, flourished, died;
great apes climbed down
from the canopy, walked
the wide savannahs on two legs.
And still you stayed, each delicate
line and curve of your shell
etched in stone, as millennium
after millennium passed.

Until, just now, the sand shifts
and your perfect form emerges.
Time collapses for us and we hear
the sea crashing on an ancient shore
at the very beginning of the world.

Patrick Connors

Country Road
for Andrew

> *"It is with the smallest brushes that the*
> *artist paints the most exquisitely*
> *beautiful pictures."* — Brother André

The air is cold, but not as cold
as it would usually be in January.
You are dressed for the journey:
jacket, touque, gloves, and boots.
The dirt road is not wet or icy,
but made uneven by tire tracks,
so you have to watch your step.

The tire tracks are not fresh
and there are no cars on the road.
There are no people, no animals–
even your cell phone is quiet.
You learn to accept the silence,
feel your breath expand your lungs,
and fully connect with the moment.

About half a kilometre ahead,
two clusters of leafless trees,
one on either side of the road,
seem to rise from patches of snow.
A mist blurs the trees like a dream
and covers what lies beyond them.
But you keep walking.

See Notes: 27

Aspire

Humility.
Patience.
Wisdom.

I have read many books on the latter, listened to stories
of the connected as well as the down-and-out
and learned what I could from them.

I have only come this far by grace.
Decades of my life have passed with nothing
but promises and the knowledge they will be fulfilled.

King Solomon was probably the wisest man who ever lived.
He had wives and influence beyond the aspirations of ordinary men.
Most of his best writing came from a spirit of deep depression.

I will try to learn from these hard-won lessons
open my eyes and mind to the new day which dawns
when I realize the true beginning of my love.

See Notes: 28

The Day Before Canada Day

A young doe, more than a yearling,
pokes her head out between two trees
adjacent to the gate of the parking lot
in front of the building where I live.

The beautiful creature furtively climbs
a shallow hill leading to the sidewalk.
To her left is a lady with a rolling suitcase.
To her right is a young boy on a bicycle.

With natural grace and instinctive fear,
the doe ambles back down the slope to shelter.
Across the street at a bus stop, I realized
I had no idea how to provide help or comfort.

Not long before I was born, wild animals
roamed free throughout this part of town.
The street immediately north of the one
on which I live is called Huntingwood.

In the high rise aspiration
for hastily erected concrete and glass
amidst the cacophony of constant traffic
the presence of a deer seems out of place.

See Notes: 29

Ron Chase

Longing

my pen
longs to write
simple secrets

for you
to place on your tongue
and whisper to yourself
when you are alone

when you most need to hear
what I am not saying

when you most need
to place another scrap
in your shoebox

at the back of your closet
where no one ever sees

For Lottie on Queen St

today you wore long sleeves
even in this hate filled heat

you sometimes dress in sunset
and I see you listening
to your music
as you make your way home
at the end of the day

lately your clothes look
like cloud cover

I will call you Lottie
I don't really know why

your arms no longer swing as you walk
there is no music left in your ears

your eyes pass the people in your way
and pull you along so you don't get lost

I fear one day soon
you won't be there
as I drive by

Your Grave

your grave stands neglected
the raised letters
on the soft stone
that once spoke your name
have all but
been erased
by the hard breath
of time and the tears
of those who used to visit
and lay lilies
in the warm spring sun

no one comes to cry anymore
no one bring flowers
on your birthday

the grass has grown tall
the sandy soil that blankets you
has sunken like an old man's eyes

now your marker only shows
where someone long ago placed
an empty shell they once loved

Sandra Davies

Another Ending
in loving memory of my father and my brother Tim

I'm living by the lake now, just your cup of tea.
It's perfect for a boat like the one you built
in our small garage when I was still a kid.
Remember how the neighbours came,
turned to one another, nudging, laughing –
He'll never wrap it up. But you did.

You could build a log house like we did when
Tim was ten. You taught him well to haul
huge logs, hammer spikes, work hard
just like a man. My job was finding *chuckies*,
little stones we stuffed in fine cracks of the fireplace
made from rocks we found down by the lake.

I have grandkids who would love the songs you used to sing
for us– *The Russian Lullaby*, the sad, sad *Hobo Song*
and then, when we were drifting off, the *Goldmine in the Sky*.
You could spin your tales about the Great Depression,
selling French newspapers on the streets of Montreal,
cooking up potatoes thirty ways.

You taught us how to swim, flip a canoe, make maple fudge.
I can still make a bonfire better than most, troll for pickerel,
sing in four parts at the same time. How I long to see you
with the bandy legs your Glasgow pappy handed down, dancing
wild and laughing down the hallway – before the pain,
the never-ending drink, the strangled tears.

We could lift our faces, shuffle around a bit. Forgive.

See Notes: 30

Bertha's Chair

Bertha sits in her usual chair,
nobody else ever settles there,
in a seat with fine upholstery
starting to sag just a little bit,
exactly like Bertha's' bottom.
Eighty years old now, she has
just fed her grownup offspring,
also her grandkids, and the cat
who is grooming his whiskers.
Her family drives from the city
whenever they can– so busy!
And now they're quite ready
to head for home, stuffed with
roast turkey and a perfectly
crusted apple cinnamon pie.

Bertha will tidy, but sits in her
special chair, watches, recalling
when Henry was there –hugging
and kissing, dancing with kids,
drying the dishes, plunking her
into her comfy perch with a laugh,
saving the last sweet song for her.
Bertha gets up, waves them all
down the road to the highway,
clears the table, heads upstairs
holding tight to the railing, up to
the room with the big feather bed.
She puts on her flannel nightie,
climbs in, shouts *Dammit Henry*,
weeps quietly into the dark.

Trilogy for Joanne

In loving memory of Joanne Page, poet

1. Revelation

In my mind, she strides
quickly, barely contained,
into the hushed business
of the old library

In my mind, a face flushed,
pale hair in damp disarray,
a smile to crack open your heart.

She was, that day, like sunlight
in a dark place. A sudden infusion
of heart heat.

2. Summer, With Cherries

Summer, spitting cherry pits
over the railing into the lavender
at the edge of her garden,

nipping around the small hard centres,
propelling them by quick flips of the tongue
with the gleeful satisfaction of six-year-olds,
mouths stained gloriously purple.

We are laughing and lazy in the sunshine,
practicing for the newly established
"Long Distance Spitting Prize"
(the last tumbler of her ginger lemonade),

speaking inconsequential silliness,
jockeying for the favorite wicker armchair
on the patio when someone gets up to
grab another fistful for the launch.

I just love this, she laughs,
flinging cherry pits to the flowers
with my buddies.

3. A New Canvas

The colours have changed,
scarlet, emerald, periwinkle vanished.
Now pastels soften, glow,
the gentle pink of seashells –
and silver glaze, matte, muted,
but silver – no mistake

The face is parchment,
scrubbed clean, a slight flush
on newly chiseled cheek bones,
blue eyes watchful, seeking;
damp white tendrils blanket
chemo's naked leavings.

A hospital bed is sketched here –
high, functional, head raised
under soft pale yellow pillows,
slim steel poles of intravenous drips –
electrolytes, morphine, salt from the sea.

A lone chair stands empty,
ready to paint yourself in.
So you do. And it is finished now –
a tiny woman lying in her bed,
a friend on a wooden chair
holding her hand.

Sarah Emtage

Phoenix Feather

I stole a feather from a phoenix,
and it seldom gives me grief.
First it shimmers in the sunlight,
then it changes like a leaf
turns from violet into silver,
then from silver into gold,
then igniting into fire,
then to ashes, grey and cold,
then I sweep it all together,
and I make a little pile,
and I rearrange my papers,
and I wait a little while
till it rises from the ashes,
and I take it up again,
and continue writing stories
with my phoenix-feather pen.

See Notes: 31

Octopus City

The octopi occupy subaquatic citadels
and ring their underwater bells
from towers in the deep,
and I can hear them as I sleep.

In a dream I wander out,
and see the sea
as black as ink.

I shiver and grin
at the moon on its skin,
then dive in,
and sink,
and sink,
and sink.

I open my eyes
and blink in surprise.
The city below is aglow
in the dark of the depths.

There are dangers dwelling in the deep
but as I dive down in my sleep
I am kept safe from all possible harms
by strong and squishy octopus arms.

Paper Crown

All I have is a paper crown,
but when I lay it down at Your feet
all my incompleteness
is suddenly complete,
and this crown that would have wilted
in the damp or in the rain
has turned to solid gold and will
eternally remain
a witness to Your glory,
and Your mercy, and Your grace,
that have brought a paper pauper here
to see You face to face.

See Notes: 32

Sarah Wells

Time and time again

Time and time again
it wrenches my heart
stiffens corners
bloods running cold

Whispers of insanity reason with uncertainty
as thy wisdom shapes
north
my sword slices
slices, into its core

wicked words left behind
thy soul trembles into peace
Forever my love
love,
Be gone

Words from a Bartender

must be ok to be watched,
Bartenders' essence oozing through motions
she/he twists thy wrists and bolts in and around,
wrapping one's body to the rhythm
must keep up

conveys a mirrored resemblance of the devil best in action
pouring spirits down throats, as cash pukes in your face

scared to admit,
one of the worlds profits
occurs,
the veil of satin himself,
the crisis of drinking,
and outcomes to blame

Dawn appears

Dawn appears
Hold down your tears
Fairytales speaking codes
Codes, erupted mindsets
Mindset rattled,
Rattled, by his own perception
A mere illusion
depth of reality found
in the midst of this pollution

Sue Bracken

Honking on the Threshold of Sleep

Winter is the cruelest season   for insomniacs

No longer can we skinny dip
with the midnight geese
or float in the moon's rippled twin

We're honking at the threshold of warmth
a blanket jujitsu where no position wins

E-read to triple vision
follow headlights as silent lightning
across the ceiling

These are useless hours
Come dawn I'll just be stupid

But today!   Today!   I am saved!!
Today Pantone announced the colour of the year!!!

The gutters of 'nothing happens'
fill with meaning
all in one colour!!

AI proclaims *Viva Magenta* 18-1750
our saving grace

All those previously confusing life messages
will now be perfectly clear and pinkish
        Everyone in leather
        No white after Labour Day
        Shorter hair is age appropriate

We insomniacs can now dwell
where blue fades to red
honking at the threshold
of no assigned wavelength

Now we can daydream
of Barbies and bridesmaids and our university selves
all in one magenta fog!

Viva la revolution!   Viva la dictated colour!

Viva   the alarm clock
Honking on the threshold of sleep

Boiling Beauties
after Starfish by Eleanor Lerman

This is what rain does
It takes you to the brink
    brings you to your knees   in the lake
    fully clothed   oblivious
    all to capture a tiny explosion

Your ever loving man
    suspends a towel over you and your camera

Life gives you a photography course
Rain gives you 20 blank shots
    You recalibrate

You   your beloved   camera   towel   again

Rain drenches all but head and camera
Whole generations of fish are summoned to stare
    You wonder- is this a message?
    and
    What is a raindrop to a fish?

You want to stand here forever
    feel the melt on your skin
    hear each plop
    witness the bounce and sink of water on water
    catch even one

More blanks
Are you old enough to appreciate this challenge? Too old?

You   your amour   camera   towel   again

Rain gives you propulsive pearls
    elegant elusive
    boiling beauties

This is what rain does
    It lets your dank unworthy self
    feel lucky not smart
    Don't settle for lucky

You're already soaked

Get the shot

JUMP

("!Warning! Parachuting is a high-risk activity which may cause or result in serious injury or death" Skydive Toronto)

Your first jump mirrored your birth   a drop
into this abyss
        on a temporary cord

Somersaults   spinning beginnings
on thin fly lines
and looped rainbow silks

So new   you   and the sky
So empty

The beauty of your first freefall
first emptiness   lost to your first mother
       leaving

45 seconds of adrenaline
heading straight for the ground
at terminal velocity

The chute unfurls at 6,000 feet
       and decades pass

You had a question   still on the wing
Government revealed the stark answer
       your adoption papers
       signed in shadows   looped black ink
       the words empty   in their fullness
       A notice of no contact is in effect

The universe roars its magnitude
We roar our astronomical love

So now the sky   we   and gravity

       Pull the cord again

The sky   almighty then
Brobdingnagian now
    you are unleashed
    landing gear intact

Smiling like a maniac

Susan J. Atkinson

This Love Poem Is for You
(for Anthony)

For you who sat at the bar in a downtown club.
For you who willingly accepted my spontaneous
tequila-fuelled fearless kiss.

For you who convinced me to remarry
that late December night when soft snow
settled in halos on streetlights below,
whose winter glow snuck through frayed shades
as we wrapped presents to put under the tree.

For you who encouraged me to rise
with the pinking of the sky to reach
the dangling string of a dream
and to hold it long enough to believe it.

For you who held me through loss,
lifted me through joy, anchored my way,
surprised me with the small things —
a favourite drink, a favourite book,
a late-night cheese-and-onion sandwich.

For you whose touch is heat and keeps me young.

See Notes: 33

This Past Month

As spiders waken
and their webs string
from gate post to post,
catching me in the early hours,
I lose things. My keys, my purse,
your parents, unexpectedly.

Our youngest daughter
collects small pebbles,
curled bark of birch trees,
rocks with eyes,
small things to bury loss.
We, too, look for ways.

We camp by our favourite lake,
seek comfort in early summer —
how sun darts between ripples of water,
how a heron lands close to shore,
strutting in the shallows of light.

The heron stays for days.
We name it as if
a loved relative,
and when it spreads
its wings to leave,
everyone waves and fusses.

See Notes: 34

The Clock She Drew

My father reads an article on cognitive ability
in a health magazine about Alzheimer's.
Following the doctor's program
he gives my mother nothing but
protein and coconut oil at every meal.
My father, having tried many cures,
prays this could be it.

Before he starts this unusual diet
he tests my mother by having her draw a clockface.
She cradles the pencil tentatively,
as if unsure of what it does, her lack of pressure
leaving only light marks on the paper.

Her clock is not really a clock at all.

Scratches like bird prints in sand
line the middle of the page.
There is no circle.
There are no hands.
My father thinks
this is a good place to start.

Two months later
he tests her again.
My mother looks thin,
having lost weight, but
the clock face remains the same.

See Notes: 35

Wendy Jean MacLean

On A Small Patch of Green
for Shelly

On a small patch of green
just outside the hospital,
the sparrows are conferring
as they read the signs
of the clouds overhead.
These feathered medics
are accustomed to changes,
but they read the cirrus charts
with great care before they decide
to fly or stay.
They take their patient very seriously.
Most of her body has been paved over
for a parking lot.
She still breathes, but barely,
gasping through the branches of trees,
planted in memory of loved ones.
I pause and pray with the sparrows,
encouraged by their persistence.
These feathered prophets will linger
in liminal space, by the entrance, by the exit
in the small patch of green.
Their full beaks herald a future
nurtured with tiny seeds of hope.
Their songs reveal a good prognosis:
Where there is love, there is life.
Where there is life, there is love.
The entrance is also the exit.
Life moves between the realms
with great care.
This is small comfort, but enough
for the next breath.

My Father Watches the Old Fox

On his birthday my father watches
the old fox foraging
through the piles of rubbish and branches
that have washed up on the shore
after the storm

The great fox tail is ragged now
like an old sentence stripped of detail
and punctuation
It was once an exclamation point
at the end of all his adventures
now it drags behind his skinny body
as a sign of loss and shame
at what he has become

My father still sees the forest youth
in the scrawny creature
scrounging at the breakwater
they both know the expense of the seasons
of wandering and change

He sees the fox as a visitor and friend
He does not need to add drama to the wonder
of two old souls
and the stories they find
and the stories they tell
in the words washed up
after the storm

See Notes: 36

Becoming Hollow

The trees in the swamp, felled by winter storms
expose their hollowed-out trunks.
For decades, they have been the home
of creatures and bugs who drew nurture
from the vitality of their inner core,
leaving the outer rim
to disguise the tree's emptiness.
There are days I long for emptiness,
for the peace of a trusting spirit,
for the silence of a resting heart,
But the birds sing
and their fluttering interruptions
defy my ascetic pretensions.
The wind in the trees beckons,
and offers to show me a different way
of being still in the midst
of unexpected longing.
It took a hundred years for these trees to grow
and only a few decades to become hollow.
My thoughts feed a thousand creatures.
Fear, loss, love, joy worry me hollow,
but trees give me words for the loss
of my need to be full, and freedom
to trust the wind will write poems in my soul
even when I fall.

Notes and Acknowledgements

1.. Allan Briesmaster, "Toward Finding"
   Forthcoming in "Later Findings" (Ekstasis Editions, 2024).

2.. Allan Briesmaster, "Windfor"
   Previously published in "Windfor" (Ekatasis Editions, 2021).

3.. Allan Briesmaster, "Quantum Bio"
   Forthcoming in "Later Findings" (Ekstasis Editions, 2024).

4.. Bethmarie Michalska, "Sparse Paean"
   Inspired by a hymn tune ("St. George's Windsor" composed by George Job Elvey,1856), to which a Christian thanksgiving song, "Come ye thankful people come," has been previously used. The tune is number 91 at the following website: http://www.ccel.org/cceh/books/svbkhl58.html
   The capitalized "You" might be a muse, or duende (after Lorca-in translation from Deep Song and Other Prose), or whatever spirit moves one to create, or to stay alive.

5.. Billie Kearns, "Habit(at)"
   Previously published in her chapbook "Caress me if I'm Wrong."

6.. Carolyn Smart, "Revelation"
   Previously published in TNQ (Spring, 2024).

7.. Carolynn Kingyens, "The Weight of Words"
   Previously published in "The Potomac" (2009) and included in "Before the Big Bang Makes a Sound" (Kelsay Books, 2020).

8.. Carolynn Kingyens, "In Sickness"
   Previously published in "Red Eft Review" (2021) and included in "Coupling" (Kelsay Books, 2021).

9.. Carolynn Kingyens, "Elephants"
   Previously published in "Coupling" (Kelsay Books, 2021).

10.. Derek Morley, "Sweet Friend"
   Previously published in "the earthbound mind reaching" (Tellwell Publishing, 2018).

11.. Doris Fiszer, "Origins"
   Previously published in "If I Were a River" (Silver Box Publishing, 2023).

12.. Doris Fiszer, "I linger in the doorway"
   Previously published in "If I Were a River" (Silver Box Publishing, 2023).

13.. Doris Fiszer, "If I were a river"
Previously published in "If I Were a River" (Silver Box Publishing, 2023).

14.. Gwenyth M Whitford, "Mountain Majesty"
Morne Diablotin (Dee-A-blo-Tin) is Dominica's highest peak, at 4,747 feet (1,447 meters) above sea level. She is one of nine volcanoes on the self-proclaimed Nature Island.

15.. Honey Novick, "Oh, Mother Earth"
Initially published by the Hague Appeal for Peace, an education branch of the United Nations, NYC.

16.. Honey Novick, "J. Edgar"
"J. Edgar" is a 2011 film directed, co-produced and scored by Clint Eastwood. It stars Leonard DiCaprio as the first head of the United States" Federal Bureau of Investigation who lasted for nearly 50 years. He was the most prominent anti-Communist in the USA (albeit during McCarthyism). After his death, it was revealed that he abused his power using the Bureau to harass, threaten and amass secret files and collect evidence using illegal means against activists, political dissenters, and political leaders. Bibliography: Wikipedia

On March 9, 1954, Edward R. Morrow wrote: This is no time for men who oppose Senator McCarthy's methods to keep silent, or for those who approve. We can deny our heritage and our history, but we cannot escape responsibility for the result. There is no way for a citizen of a republic to abdicate his responsibilities. As a nation we have come into our full inheritance at a tender age. We proclaim ourselves, as indeed we are, the defenders of freedom, wherever it continues to exist in the world, but we cannot defend freedom abroad by deserting it at home."

17.. Honey Novick, "J. Edgar"
Previously published in "Bob Dylan, My Rabbi (How Does It Feel?)" (Secret Handshake Publishing, 2022).

18.. Jane Macdonald, "In Memoriam"
Previously published in the Wellington Times (Nov 9, 2022).

19.. Jane Macdonald, "Two Years ago a Trumpeter Swan was Frozen in the Harbour"
Previously published in "Leap: a chapbook in memory of Lesley Strutt" (League of Canadian Poets, 2022).

20.. Jason Heroux, "from From There, The Visitor"
Inspired from a trip to Greece in 2022, a poetic sequence titled "From There, the Visitor" was created. Included here; three segments from that sequence.

21.. Kate Marshall Flaherty, "Poplar Grove"
        First published in "Worth More Standing: Poets and Activists Pay Homage to Trees" (Edited by Pat Lowther, Caitlin Press, 2022).

22.. Kate Marshall Flaherty, "Sel"
        First published in "Titch" (Piquante Press, 2023).

23.. Kate Marshall Flaherty, "White on Green"
        First published in "Digging" (Aeolus House, 2022).

24.. Meg Freer, "Pitch-Perfect Dreams"
        Previously published in "The Daughter's Grimoire" (Issue 4, February 2024).

25.. Meg Freer, "Seeds of Control"
        Previously published in "Tiny Seed Literary Journal" (April 18, 2023).

26.. Meg Freer, "Interwoven"
        Previously published in "COG" (Issue 9 online, Feb 2018).

27.. Patrick Connors, "Country Road"
        Previously published in "Over the Garden Fence" (Feb 2023). And reprinted in "Poetry & Performance Volume 1" by Green Mountains Writers Group.

28.. Patrick Connors, "Aspire"
        Previously published by "Agape Review" (Oct 2021).

29.. Patrick Connors, "The Day Before Canada Day"
        Previously published in "Canadian Stories" (October/November 2022 issue). And featured on the League of Canadian Poets Poetry Pause; July 14, 2023.

30.. Sandra Davis, "Another Ending"
        Previously published in "Giacometti's Girl" (Cormorant Books, 2018).

31.. Sarah Emtage, "Phoenix Feather"
        Previously published in "Paperscape" (2018).

32.. Sarah Emtage, "Paper Crown"
        Previously published in "Paperscape" (2018).

33.. Susan J. Atkinson, "This Love Poem Is for You"
        Previously published in "all things small" (Silver Bow Publishing, 2024).

34.. Susan J. Atkinson, "This Past Month"
    Previously published in "all things small" (Silver Bow Publishing, 2024).

35.. Susan J. Atkinson, "The Clock She Drew"
    Previously published in "all things small" (Silver Bow Publishing, 2024).

36.. Wendy Jean MacLean, "My Father Watches the Old Fox"
    Previously published in an Ontario Poetry Society chapbook.

Contributors:

Abbie Miolée is a Kingston-based activist, artist, poet, and musician from Atlanta, Georgia. She experiences art as the practice of giving emotions a body to dance in the hearts of others, and through this practice, explores the connective nature of life. Abbie finds meaning in community involvement as it reminds her that she is part of a whole which is greater than the sum of its parts. Always gravitated toward wilderness, she is fascinated by plants and fungi, and how trees communicate underground through mycelial networks. Abbie believes that the sacred and secular are two sides of the same coin and her intention as an artist and scientist is to harmonize the two perspectives.

Alanna Veitch is a PhD student in Gender Studies at Queen's University with a master's degree in health science. She is also a sister, daughter, activist, former professional dancer, and emerging scholar and writer whose body insists on moving differently. Currently, Alanna's work touches on themes of disability, female embodiment, temporality, crisis, and hope. Her creative work has recently been accepted for publication in *Devour: Art & Lit Canada*. Her academic work has been published in *Critical Inquiry*, and submitted to *Feminist Futures* special issue in *Gender, Work & Organization*. Alanna assembles herself through writing, using poetry as a way of relating and being in the world.

Allan Briesmaster is a poet, freelance editor and publisher who has been active on the Toronto-area literary scene for many years. With yet a tenth book, *Toward Finding* (Guernica Editions, 2024), coming out soon, the most recent of his nine books of poetry are *The Long Bond: Selected and New Poems* (Guernica Editions, 2019) and *Windfor* (Ekstasis Editions, 2021). Allan was one of the organizers of the Art Bar Poetry Reading Series in the 1990s until 2002, and was a partner in Quattro Books from 2006 to 2017. Currently, he runs his own small press, Aeolus House, specializing in limited-edition books of poetry. A Life Member of the League of Canadian Poets, he has read his work, given talks, and hosted readings and book launches at venues from St. John's to Victoria, as well as online. He lives in Thornhill, Ontario

Amy Cadman is a Kingston-based theatre practitioner with a keen interest in immersive exploration and storytelling. She has previously participated in Bruce Kauffman's open mic readings during the pandemic. These are her first published poems. Thanks for the confidence to submit it, Bruce and fellow workshop poets!

Anne Archer (aka Archer Lundy) is a musician and poet who lives on unceded Algonquin Territory near Sharbot Lake, Ontario. She is the author of three books of poetry, the last of which, *EMMALINE/EVANGELINE* (Woodpecker Lane Press, 2023) takes as its inspiration the paintings of her mother-in-law, Evangeline Phillips Murray. Anne's recent poetry appears in *Devour, Pinhole, Anti-Heroin Chic, Autumn Sky Poetry, The Lothlorien Poetry Journal, Poetry Pause,* and *The Avalon Literary Review.* Her poem, 'The Man from U.N.C.L.E.,' is forthcoming from *In the Mood Magazine.*

Anne Graham (aka Anergy) lives in Kingston. She only started sharing her writing in 2012. Anne has been published in five anthologies and has written 5 yearly chapbooks. She has also enjoyed spoken word poetry, and attended quite a few Slam events. Her favourite events each year are our annual Artfest Poets @ Artfest summer poetry festival, and the 100,000 Poets for Change happenings. Anne also writes poetry often to read during services at Kingston Unitarian Fellowship. She gives many thanks to her friend Bruce Kauffman for his encouragement and his advice given to her since they met in 2012. Anne aka Anergy 2023.

Armand Garnet Ruffo is an Anishinaabe writer from Treaty # 9 territory in northern Ontario. A recipient of an Honourary Life Membership Award from The League of Canadian Poets and the Latner Canada Writers' Trust Poetry Prize, he is recognized as a major contributor to both Indigenous literature and Indigenous literary scholarship in Canada. His publications *Norval Morrisseau: Man Changing Into Thunderbird* (2014) and *Treaty#* (2019) were finalists for Governor General Literary Awards. A new book, *The Dialogues: the Song of Francis Pegahmagabow* will be published in 2024. He now lives in Kingston.

Bethmarie Michalska likes to sing, write, and experience trees along with other sentient beings. Her poems have appeared in *Quarry, Queen's Undergraduate Review, Lake Effect 6, That Not Forgotten, Synergy, Canada's 150th: A Poetic Anthology, Inspired Heart for Teens* & its second volume: *Identity and Diversity,* online at 'The Poetry Blackboard' as well as other places. Individual works include a chapbook, *North Superior Bardo,* and solo & group poetry readings around Kingston, including the Kingston Public Library and the Memorial Centre Farmer's Market. Otherwise, she's had a career as a clinical psychologist and adjunct professor at Queen's University in health sciences. She welcomes reader's interest and can be reached at: beth.michalska@gmail.com

Billie Kearns (aka Billie the Kid) is a K'ai Taile Dené and Nehiyaw spoken word poet and storyteller. Originally from Yellowknife, NT, she now resides in Kingston, ON, the traditional home of the Haudenosaunee, Anishinaabe, and Huron-Wendat. Billie is Head of Research and Development for Qubit Systems where she designs instrumentation for biological and environmental science. She simultaneously holds an active poetic practice – she performs and holds workshops at events across Turtle Island both in-person and virtually. Her poetry breathes life into narratives as she explores relationships with family, friends, food, and the dynamic nature of dreams. Billie explores what it means to be in relation with our stories, and what it means to share them.

Brent Raycroft's poetry has appeared in a variety of magazines, journals and anthologies, including *Best of Walrus Poetry* (2013) and *The Best of the Best Canadian Poetry: Tenth Anniversary Edition* (2017). He lives north of Kingston Ontario at the southern edge of Algonquin traditional territory and the northern edge of Haudenosaunee traditional territory.

Carma Niceforo is a Kingston poet, storyteller and Beekeeper. Carma's poetry is inspired by overcoming the odds using Fairy Tale imagery and themes. When she's not writing poetry or leading Ghost Tours at Fort Henry, you can find her having tea in the company of several thousand of her closest friends, her bees.

Carolyn Smart has written six collections of poetry including *Careen*, *Hooked*, and *The Way to Come Home* (all from Brick Books). A section of her memoir *At the End of the Day* (Penumbra Press) won 1st prize in the CBC Literary Contest, Non-Fiction category. For three decades she taught Creative Writing at Queen's University. She is the founder of the Bronwen Wallace Award for Emerging Writers, poetry editor for McGill-Queen's Press, and since 2021 has worked as an editor and mentor for emerging writers.

Carolynn Kingyens was born and raised in Northeast Philadelphia. She is the author of two poetry collections, *Before the Big Bang Makes a Sound* (2020) and *Coupling* (2021), both published by Kelsay Books. In addition to poetry, Kingyens writes essays, book and film reviews, micro and short fiction. Her two short stories "Bye Bye, Miss American Pie" and "The Invitation" won Best of Fiction by Across the Margin, a Brooklyn arts & culture webzine and podcast, for 2021 and 2023, respectively. In 2021, Carolynn and her family moved to Canada from Brooklyn, NY.

Catherine Jones was born and raised in Toronto, Ontario. She started writing before age 10, but because she pursued a career as a registered nurse writing took a back seat. Catherine started writing poetry again in retirement, and presently resides in Kingston, Ontario.

David Blaikie grew up in rural Nova Scotia. He was a reporter for many years on Parliament Hill and had a second career in the Canadian labor movement. He has published four volumes of poetry. His most recent, *A Season In Lowertown*, won first prize in the Don Gutteridge Canadian poetry awards. It was published in 2022 by *Wet Ink Books*. An earlier collection won the inaugural chapbook award of the *Tree Reading Series* in Ottawa. David lives in Kanata with his long-time partner, Susan Rosidi, and a gray rescue cat named Billie.

David Malone was born in Toronto but now lives in Kingston with his family. Some of his poems have appeared in previous anthologies issued by Hidden Brook Press, including *That Not Forgotten* and *The Beauty of Being Elsewhere*.

Derek Morley says he "make grammatical errors, and not always by accident." He has been spotted jaywalking. His poetry binds whimsy to requirement. He is obsessed with pens. He finds them abandoned on the avenue. Don't even worry about his first book of poetry *Cuba Diaries*, self-published in 2013, written in 2005. It smells of cigars and has a mojito stain on the cover. To be fair, *the earthbound mind rising* 2016 deals with travels in India. It's slightly better. It has pictures. His new book *One Hour More*, is a poetic unraveling of the heart. Published in January 2024, it's now available on Amazon and book-stores everywhere.

Doris Fiszer is an Ottawa poet. Her publications include *If I Were a River* and *Locked in Different Alphabets*, which was a finalist for the 2021 Archibald Lampman Award. She has published two chapbooks, *The Binders* and *Sasanka* (Wild Flower). Her poems have appeared in a variety of journals and anthologies across Canada and the United States.

Elizabeth Greene has published three books of poetry, a short story chapbook, and a novel. She has edited/co-edited six books, most recently *The Dowager Empress: Poems by Adele Wiseman* (Inanna, 2019). In a previous incarnation, she taught English at Queen's and was a founder of Women's Studies (now Gender Studies). Her poems here are part of a ten-poem sequence, "Tree Story."

Eric Folsom: Originally from Massachusetts, Eric Folsom attended universities in Montreal and Halifax before moving to Kingston in 1974. In the 80s and 90s, he published a literary 'zine called *Next Exit*, while running a reading series known as Cargo Kulture, usually at The Sleepless Goat on Princess Street. His most recent chapbook, *Lift Bridge*, takes its title from the lift bridge on the LaSalle Causeway in downtown Kingston.

Gwenith M Whitford grew up in Kingston, Ontario, Canada and then lived in other places for 35 years. She returned to her hometown in 2016, after having resided in Dominica, the self-proclaimed Nature Island for two decades. While living in this beautiful locale, she became inspired to write poetry while teaching English Literature to senior high school students. Some of her poetry creations have been published in anthologies and a few have won awards. She is currently working on her first chapbook. When winter sets in, she escapes to her beloved adopted country whenever possible, where her creative yearnings bear fruit. A poem of hers included here, 'Mountain Majesty,' placed third in the Dominica Independence 2023 Literary Competition, English Poetry category.

Honey Novick, a 2024 nominee for Poet Laureate of Ontario, a 2024 Dovercourt Good Neighbour Awardee, a 2023 Outstanding Neighbour Awardee, and is the 2022 Community Hero in the Arts winner, St. Paul's Riding, Ontario. She is a member of the League of Canadian Poets, The Writer's Union of Canada, Poetry in Voice, and SOCAN. She is the 2019 CSARN (Canadian Senior Artists Resource Network) Mentor Awardee, and the 2022 and 2023 Writer's Union of Canada Mentor Awardee. She has 8 CDs, LPs, and 10 books of poetry to her name. Her work has appeared in numerous anthologies and magazines, and she has been published internationally. Her complete catalogue of poetry books and CDs was purchased for the permanent collection, National Art Gallery of Canada/Ottawa/General Idea Reading Room. "Bob Dylan, My Rabbi" was purchased for the Robarts Library. University of Toronto.

Jane Macdonald. A recipient and a finalist of the Janice Colbert Poetry Award , Jane Macdonald is at work on a manuscript of poems of place marked by disappearance and loss.

Jason Heroux lives in Kingston, Ontario, works at ServiceOntario, and lives with his wife Soheir and their two cats, Pablo and Neruda. He is the author of four books of poetry: *Memoirs of an Alias* (2004), *Emergency Hallelujah* (2008), *Natural Capital* (2012) and *Hard Work Cheering Up Sad Machines* (2016). His most recent publication is the short story collection *Survivors of the Hive* (Radiant Press, 2023). A collection of prose poems, *Like a Trophy From the Sun*, is forthcoming this fall with Guernica Editions. He was the Poet Laureate for the City of Kingston from 2019 to 2022.

Jen Frankel is a poet, author, musician, and lover of the arts. Her work has appeared in publications as diverse as *Amazing Stories* magazine and the *Griffin*, and she has received awards for her plays, screenplays, poetry, and fiction including second prize in the International 3-Day Novel Writing Competition for her memoir *Sincere Flattery*. She hosts the long-running *Write On! Write Now* open mic in Toronto and makes her home in the Steel City, Hamilton.

Jennifer Londry is the author of three books of poetry. She lives in the limestone city.

Jennifer Verardi. Born in Timmins, Ontario, Jennifer is an actor, a writer, lyricist, musician and a designer; she is a storyteller at heart. She began writing poetry in her childhood because it helped her to express herself and the multitudes of emotions she experienced as she tried to comprehend the world. As an adult, she is most often found on stage in the Kingston area as an actor, and recently in the Hastings area as a musician. Jennifer is beyond grateful to have found the Poet community of Kingston in 2019 as she believes "it has saved me time and time again—and I am so looking forward to what is yet to come!"

Joel Giroux has just recently relocated to Kingston after 35 or more years in Toronto and environs. He has worked as an Intervenor with Persons with Deaf-Blindness, as an English teacher at George Brown College in Toronto, and in the last decade, shifted over into the trades, joining his brothers as an hydronics installer. He has worked the auto desk at Canadian Tire, pushing tires, but you can find him now at Novel Idea, pushing books. He also works as a freelance tutor, editor, and ghost writer. He has appeared in *Anthos, UC Review, Trinity College Review* and, most recently, in the Pulp issue of *The Quarantine Review*. He's a grandpa who plays piano and bass to start and end each day.

Judith Popiel is an interdisciplinary independent artist who writes poetry, short stories and articles about dance and theatre. She loves to dance and work on mixed media art canvases in her spare time.

Kate Marshall Flaherty has published eight books of poetry, most recently *Titch* (Piquante Press 2023) and *Digging* (Aeolus House, 2022). She was shortlisted for the Mitchell Poetry Prize 2021, *Arc*'s Poem of the Year 2019, and the Gwendolyn MacEwen Poetry Prize 2018. She has been published in numerous Canadian and international journals such as *The Literary Review of Canada, American Academy of Poets, Contemporary Verse 2, Vallum, Grain, Room, untethered* and *Trinity Review*. She is a monthly host at the Art Bar, Canada's longest running poetry series. She writes spontaneous "Poems of the Extraordinary Moment" (P.O.E.M.s) for charity, in person and online, and guides StillPoint Writing and Poetry Editing Circles in person and online. See her performance poetry at https://katemarshallflaherty.ca

Kelsey Newman Reed is an artist, published poet, and has always been passionate about the arts. She has spent many years crafting poems and illustrations that tell stories of the trees, the moon, (our) hands, and the water. If she isn't able to write about nature or draw it, Kelsey will often spend time taking photos of the shadows the sun makes, and how the plants dance within it. Her work often attempts to feel serene, calm, and soft.

Leslie Saunders lives in Kingston, where she divides her time, somewhat unequally, between word wrangling, trying to corral her unruly stable of saxophones, and having deep philosophical discussions with her dog about which one of them should make the decisions on the agility course. She will be reading a selection of both vintage and newer work.

Louise Carson lives in a bungalow surrounded by gardens in rural Quebec. She paid it off by teaching music. Now she just writes. She has published three books of poetry: *The Truck Driver Treated for Shock* (haiku, Yarrow Press, 2024); *Dog Poems* (Aeolus House, 2020); and *A Clearing* (Signature Editions, 2015). Poems have been selected for *Best Canadian Poetry* in 2013, 2021 and 2024. She also writes mysteries and historical fiction. Her two latest novels are: *The Cat Looked Back* (Signature, 2023); and *Third Circle* (land/sea press, 2022).

Madison Cuddon is a Kingston-based writer. Her poems delve into the complexities of love and passion– and explore the ups and downs that come with them. With inspirations such as Lana del Rey and Sylvia Plath, Madison navigates the tragedy of romance and girlhood.

Maria Mitea says, "I was born in a family of ten children, in the south of Moldova (former Russian Republic). Parents taught us to love people, our roots, and our soulful nature. Mother always stayed by our side. She cooked tasty food and baked bread. From her, I learned to write poetry. From my father, I learned to respect the land and the hard work in the fields. With brothers and sisters, we studied together and shared the joy of playing. My grandmother had a big cherry orchard, plum trees, and apples. We spent lots of time there climbing and picking the fruit. In the culture, we were taught to embrace dance, to cry, to laugh, and the goodwill of life. In the family, we learned that the beauty of life is hidden in its simplicity. I believe that it is the same in poetry. I immigrated to Canada in 2001."

Meg Freer grew up in Montana and now teaches piano and writes in Kingston, Ontario, on traditional Anishinaabe and Haudenosaunee lands. Her writing has appeared in journals such as *Arc Poetry*, *Queen's Quarterly*, and *Eastern Iowa Review*, and she is co-author of a poetry chapbook, *Serve the Sorrowing World with Joy* (Woodpecker Lane Press, 2020) and author of two other chapbooks. She holds a Graduate Certificate in Creative Writing with Distinction from Humber School of Writers.

Mike Madill's poems have been published across Canada, including in *The Antigonish Review*, *Event*, *The Fiddlehead* and *The New Quarterly*. He was shortlisted for Freefall's 2019-'20 Poetry Contest, and an Honourable Mention in the inaugural 2021-'22 Don Gutteridge Poetry Award Contest earned him publication of his debut collection, *The Better Part of Some Time*. When not writing, Mike pursues freelance editing, and has also taken turns as a social worker, computer analyst, and home contractor. He holds a B.A. in Psychology from York University, and has a tendency to daydream out windows.

Nathalie Sorensen is enjoying her retirement, spending time with friends and family, gardening, taking photographs, reading and writing poetry. She taught English at St. Lawrence College for 27 years, and is the mother of three grown sons.

Patrick Connors' first chapbook, *Scarborough Songs*, was released by Lyricalmyrical Press in 2013, and charted on the Toronto Poetry Map. Other publication credits include: The Toronto Quarterly; Spadina Literary Review; Sharing Spaces; Tamaracks; and Tending the Fire. His first full collection, *The Other Life*, was released in 2021 by Mosaic Press. His new chapbook, *Worth the Wait*, was released in 2023 by Cactus Press. His next collection is forthcoming.
Facebook: https://www.facebook.com/patrick.j.connors.3
Twitter: https://twitter.com/81912CON
Instagram: https://www.instagram.com/patjtconnors/

Ron Chase is a Kingston area poet whose work can be read in various literary journals and anthologies, and he can often be found late at night hunched over a tiny black desk writing truths that hide during the day, or testing new work at open mic nights and literary events.

Sandra Davies is a retired palliative care nurse who grew up in Toronto and has been writing what she called "my pomes" since she was a kid. She graduated from the Univ. of Toronto with a BScN in Nursing, and for the next 40 years practiced her profession in Toronto, Madhya Pradesh India, and Kingston, her home since 1989. After retiring she fell headlong into writing. She's had poems appear in literary magazines & anthologies. *Giacometti's Girl* is her first book, published in 2018, and she has just finished a chapbook about her adventures in India, and a manuscript with which she is still wrestling, entitled *Dancing on Sore Feet*. She is also a mum of two adult sons, and two well– loved daughters-in-law and a grandma of four perfect grandchildren.

Sarah Emtage is a poet, playwright, sculptor, and library technician in Kingston Ontario. She has written two poetry books, *Paperscape* and *The Second Rate Poetry of S. M. Emtage*, a picture book called *The Time Wager*, and a radio play series called *Sound Castle*. She is working on a children's poetry collection called *Clay Castle* and a radio adaptation of *The Princess and The Goblin*. She is currently keeping a spider plant alive. See more of what she's up to at Instagram: Scribblore_Poetry, or Scribblore.com

Sarah Wells, a creative entrepreneur, is unconventional in her written and sung abilities. 2020 awardee of CSARN mentorship program and published by the award wining Friendly Spike Theatre Band, Hidden Book Press, and The Secret Handshake. Sarah pulls in on grief and realistic life twists in her writing, channels her inner poet in times of reflection.

Sue Bracken's work has appeared in: Angel House Press (NationalPoetryMonth.ca), *GUEST* [a journal of guest editors], *Hart House Review, Dusie, Touch the Donkey, WEIMAG, The New Quarterly, Another Dysfunctional Cancer Poem Anthology* (Mansfield Press), *The Totally Unknown Writer's Festival 2015: Stories* (Life Rattle Press) and elsewhere. *When Centipedes Dream* is her debut poetry collection (Tightrope Books, 2018). Her chapbook *27* is forthcoming from Battleaxe Press. Sue lives and writes in Toronto in a home overthrown by artists and animals.

Susan J. Atkinson is an award-winning poet. Recently, she received honourable mention in the New Quarterly's 2023 Nick Blatchford Occasional Verse Content and was longlisted for the 2023 Ruth and David Lampe Poetry Award. Her work has appeared widely in journals, anthologies, and online. Her debut poetry collection, *The*

Marta Poems, was published in 2020 by Silver Bow Publishing. Her second collection, *all things small*, will appear in spring 2024. See www.susanjatkinson.com

Wendy Jean MacLean. A love of words and the spiritual practice of writing poetry drew Wendy into the community of other spiritual writers, ancient and contemporary, as a minister with the United Church of Canada. Her words emerge from deep listening to mystery and beauty. // Her work has been published in several anthologies and journals. She has 3 books of poetry. The most recent is *On Small Wings*, a Don Gutteridge poetry award winner. Her work has been commissioned by several composers and sung internationally. Her poem, 'Before You Even Knew', with music by Dr. Mark Sirett, was commissioned for the National Unison Choir Festival in Halifax in May to commemorate the 2S LGBTQ+ purge by the federal government during the 1950s to the 1990s. Wendy is a spiritual director in the tradition of soul friends and contemplative reflection.

Miguel Ángel Olivé Iglesias

Professor Miguel Ángel Olivé Iglesias graduated from the Teacher Training College of Holguín and is now an Associate Professor of Holguín University with a Master's degree in English. He has published more than thirty books as author/coauthor, editor/coeditor, literary reviewer, proofreader and translator. He is the V.P. of the Canada Caribbean Literary Alliance, the Editor-in-chief of the official CCLA flagship magazine *The Ambassador* and a translator for the "CanLit in Translation" Series for WIB.

Professor Olivé has published numerous books with SandCrab Books, Hidden Brook Press, Wet Ink Books and QuodSermo Publishing. Among some of those books are his reviews and essays book, *In a Fragile Moment: A Landscape of Canadian Poetry* (HBP); *A Shower of Warm Light: Reviews and Essays on Canadian Poetry* (QSP); *Five Canadian Poets: Analytical Essays on, James Deahl, John B. Lee, Don Gutteridge, Glen Sorestad, A. F. Moritz* (QSP); and *On the Breeze of Canadian Literature: International Reviews and Essays* (QSP). His CanLit book *The Canadian Poet Who Wrote Himself Whole: Revealing the Poetics of Don Gutteridge*, was published in 2022, with QSP.

In 2024 he also published his academic book, *A Cuban Professor's Journey in FLT: Thirty-Five Years of Teaching English as a Foreign Language* published with QSP. With WIB, as part of the "CanLit in Translation" series he published *When the Muses Visit: My Twenty Favourite John B. Lee Poems. An Annotated Selection / Cuando las musas visitan: Mis veinte poemas favoritos de John B. Lee. Una selección comentada* and *A Grove of Poetry / Una Huerta de Poemas*. His QSP book of CanLit essays, *The Light Candling the Mind. A Journey across Canadian Literature. Reviews and Essay* will be released in 2024.

Bruce Kauffman

Bruce Kauffman is a poet and editor living in Kingston, Ontario. He began writing poetry his first year in university in 1968. He credits five episodes in his life regarding poetry that were for him pivotal. The first at age 14, in 1965 after seeing the film *Doctor Zhivago* in a theatre, as he walked out, for the first time in his life he truly believed he would someday be a poet. The second, one day in the spring of 1968, his English teacher required each student to write a full poem in class that day. The third, from fall1968-73 while in university, he spent  nearly all of his free time writing poetry. The fourth, in the early 90's, he discovered his favourite poet, W. S. Merwin, and absolutely fell in love with poetry. And fifth, again early 90's, he discovered the 'magic' in attending live readings and workshops.

Since 2013 he has authored five collections of poetry: *The Texture of Days in Ash and Leaf* (Hidden Brook Press, 2013); *a seed within* (Hidden Brook Press, 2013); *The Silence Before the Whisper Comes* (Hidden Brook Press, 2013); *an evening absence still waiting for moon* (Hidden Brook Press, 2019); and *still arriving* (Wet Ink Books, 2023). He's also had four chapbooks published. His work has appeared in a number of periodicals, journals, and anthologies in Canada and the US.

His poetry appearing in plays: *The Garbage and the Flowers* (2008), *A Moveable Feast* (2009), *Waste/Away* (2015), *Dionysus: A Celebration of Defiance* (2016), and *Rhinoceros* (2017). His words have also been on display in collaboration with visual artists: *Re-Collection* w/ Lee-Ann Taras & Andrew Sims (The Artel, Summer 2008); *Stitch and Stanza* w/ fibre artist Janet Elliot (KWF, 2014); *But 6 Moments in the all of Time* w/ Ali Dixon (Unit 115, KAC, May 2018); and *The Elm Suite* w/ Michèle LaRose (The Elm Café, Dec 2018-March 2019).

Awards: Poiesis Regional Poetry Competition (Colorado, 1995) – shortlisted; Community Creator Award (Vancouver, 2017) – won; *Who is Bruce Kauffman?* (KCFF, 2019) – a feature film highlighting poets, their poems, & poetry in Kingston; The Mayor's Arts Champion Award (Kingston, 2020); and The Don Gutteridge Poetry Award (for *still arriving*, 2022) - Honourable Mention.

Editing: Since 2012 he has edited 9 anthologies; was Board Member & Outreach Mentor for Queen's Poetry Slam (2014); Ad hoc Outreach Coordinator for QPS (2015/16); Acquisitions and Poetry Editor for Wintergreen Studios Press (2012-18); a staff writer for *Free Lit Magazine* (2017-20); and is poetry editor for *Devour: Art and Lit Canada* (since 2019).

Poetry & lit projects: *and the journey continues* – a monthly open mic reading series (originator & host, 2009-ongoing); *finding a voice* –a weekly poetry/lit related radio show on CFRC 101.9fm & cfrc.ca (original creator, producer, & host, 2010 – ongoing); *An Intuitive Writing Workshop* (facilitator, 2012-ongoing); event organizer and promoter (2013-ongoing); *Poets @ Artfest* – (organizer & host, 2015-ongoing); and *The Floating List of Calls & Events* — a free weekly 10 page newsletter of calls and events (founder/editor/publisher, 2017-ongoing).

www.ingramcontent.com/pod-product-compliance
Lightning Source LLC
Chambersburg PA
CBHW011221120626
46545CB00010B/3100